Walking the
Tightrope of Reason

❧

Walking the Tightrope of Reason

THE PRECARIOUS LIFE OF A RATIONAL ANIMAL

Robert Fogelin

OXFORD
UNIVERSITY PRESS

2003

OXFORD
UNIVERSITY PRESS

Oxford New York
Auckland   Bangkok Buenos Aires Cape Town
Chennai Dar es Salaam Delhi Hong Kong Istanbul Karachi   Kolkata
Kuala Lumpur Madrid   Melbourne Mexico City Mumbai Nairobi
São Paulo Shanghai Taipei Tokyo Toronto

Published by Oxford University Press, Inc.
198 Madison Avenue, New York, New York 10016

www.oup.com

Oxford is a registered trademark of Oxford University Press

Library of Congress Cataloging-in-Publication Data
Fogelin, Robert J.
   Walking the tightrope of reason : the precarious life of a rational
animal / Robert J. Fogelin.
      p. cm.
Includes bibliographical references and index.
   ISBN 0-19-516026-6
 1. Reason. 2. Skepticism. 3. Metaphysics. I. Title.
 BC177 .F64 2003
   128'.33—dc21

2002190897

Book design by planettheo.com

9 8 7 6 5 4 3 2 1

Printed in the United States of America
on acid-free paper

For my son, Lars Fogelin

Under a Certain Little Star

I apologize to coincidence for calling it necessity.
I apologize to necessity just in case I'm mistaken.
. . . .
I apologize to big questions for small answers.
O Truth, do not pay me too much heed.
O Solemnity, be magnanimous unto me.
Endure, mystery of existence, that I pluck out the threads
    of your train.
Accuse me not, O soul, of possessing you but seldom.
I apologize to everything that I cannot be everywhere.
I apologize to everyone that I cannot be every man and
    woman.
I know that as long as I live nothing can justify me,
because I myself am an obstacle to myself.
Take it not amiss, O speech, that I borrow weighty words,
and later try hard to make them seem light.

Wislawa Szymborska

CONTENTS

PREFACE

This thin volume is the offspring of a series of lectures I presented in 1995 as the Romanell-Phi Beta Kappa Professor of Philosophy. The award, made by the national chapter of Phi Beta Kappa, provides an opportunity for a faculty member to offer a series of lectures of general interest to members of his or her home academic community. Through its auspices, I gave three public lectures at Dartmouth College under the general title "The Precarious Life of a Rational Animal." In the process of revision, these three lectures grew into the seven chapters presented here.

The intended audience for this work, as for the original lectures, is the educated reader, but there is a second audience as well that has caused me no end of difficulties, namely, my professional philosophical colleagues, whose opinions I respect. They quite reasonably could challenge virtually everything said in this work. In the process of revising the original lectures, I found myself more and more concerned with them rather than with the original audience. What to do? In the end I decided to return to the standpoint of the original lectures and simply report how things strike me. How things strike professional philosophers—what objections they might raise—is, for the most part, not my present concern.

There is, however, a problem with this approach: I may seem to be claiming as my own ideas belonging to others. In the preface to his *Tractatus Logico-Philosophicus,* Ludwig Wittgenstein addressed this problem with the following remarkable "disclaimer":

> I do not wish to judge how far my efforts coincide with those of other philosophers. Indeed, what I have written here makes no claim to novelty in detail, and the reason why I give no sources is that it is a matter of indifference to me whether the thoughts that I have had have been anticipated by someone else.

Having said this, Wittgenstein does go on to acknowledge his indebtedness "to Frege's great works and to the writings of [his] friend Mr. Bertrand Russell." Because I am offering a similar disclaimer, let me acknowledge my own indebtednesses. They are chiefly four: the ancient Pyrrhonian skeptics as represented in the writings of Sextus Empiricus; David Hume, in particular his *Treatise of Human Nature;* Immanuel Kant, specifically the part of his *Critique of Pure Reason* entitled "Transcendental Dialectic"; and Ludwig Wittgenstein, primarily his *Philosophical Investigations.* This is not a work about these writers, nor is it an attempt to reconcile their many differences. In the spirit of Wittgenstein's disclaimer, I gladly give them credit for anything compelling in this work and take the blame for the rest.

I am greatly indebted to a number of institutions and persons for their help and encouragement in producing this work. The process began when the Dartmouth chapter of

Phi Beta Kappa nominated me to be Romanell-Phi Beta Kappa Professor of Philosophy. The national chapter of Phi Beta Kappa subsequently accepted their recommendation. Without the support of the local and national chapters of Phi Beta Kappa, this work would not have been undertaken.

During the spring of 2001 I was provided an ideal setting for completing a first draft of this work as a fellow at the Bogliasco Foundation's Ligurian Study Center for the Arts and Humanities. My research has also enjoyed generous support from Dartmouth College through its sabbaticals, senior research fellowships, and the research stipend associated with the Sherman Fairchild Professorship in the Humanities.

Starting with the public lectures given at Dartmouth College in 1995, I have presented this material to a variety of audiences. I have enjoyed the lively discussions that followed, and learned a great deal from them. I also appreciate the support and helpful suggestions of the anonymous readers for Oxford University Press. I was fortunate that Peter Ohlin and Catherine Humphries undertook the complex process of seeing this work through press. As before, I would like to thank Jane Taylor and Florence Fogelin for their editorial skills, their intelligent criticisms, and their fine ears for the English language.

Over the years, my colleague Walter Sinnott-Armstrong has served as a sounding board, a critic, sometimes an enthusiast and other times a damper for my philosophical ideas. Both directly and indirectly he has contributed to this work in many ways. My son, Lars Fogelin, deserves special note. Though not a professional philosopher—he is completing a doctoral degree in archeology—he takes philosophical issues seriously. Responding to his criticisms and suggestions has, I think, made this a less insular book. It has certainly delayed its completion—though to good effect.

TEXTS AND CITATIONS

For the sake of simplicity, I have kept the scholarly apparatus in the notes as simple as possible. Full details of the works cited are presented in the bibliography.

*Walking the
Tightrope of Reason*

&

INTRODUCTION

Our lives as rational animals are carried out under extraordinarily difficult conditions. The universe we inhabit is exceedingly—almost perversely—complex. Albert Einstein once remarked that "God is slick, but he ain't mean," but this seems less and less obvious, given the strangeness of reports coming back from the frontiers of science.[1] Such complexity and strangeness by themselves do not, however, make our lives as rational animals precarious; they simply make them hard going.

A more pressing problem arises because we as human beings are also irrational animals, unique among animals in our capacity to place faith in bizarre fictions of our own construction. That superstition—in both its institutionalized and noninstitutionalized forms—continues to dominate much of human life is both deplorable and not sufficiently deplored. Irrationality, however, is not the topic of this work, which is not concerned with forces that displace or corrupt reason from the outside. It is concerned with problems inherent in the rational enterprise, that is, problems that make reasoning itself a precarious activity.

One leading idea of this work is that reason, pursued without constraint, tends to drive us in one of two contrasting directions. The first is the way of metaphysics, which, at least in its traditional form, is an attempt to produce a purely rational (a priori) account of the unchanging, underlying structure of reality. That there must be such a structure is a demand of reason itself. The second, contrasting tendency is for reason, when driven to its limits, to undercut itself, yielding radical skepticism or radical relativism. What is surprising is that these contrasting tendencies—though seemingly poles apart—are often united in sharing an underlying commitment. Here is one example:

If there is no God, then everything is pointless.[2]

This conditional statement can be equivalently expressed as a disjunction, that is, as an either-or:

Either God exists or everything is pointless.

We are now faced with a choice. If we reject the existence of God, we are then committed to the pointlessness of the world. If, conversely, we reject the pointlessness of the world, we are then committed to the existence of God. A related principle comes from Fyodor Dostoyevsky's *Brothers Karamazov:*

If there is no God, then everything is [morally] possible.

This principle is intended to force a choice between religion and moral nihilism.

It seems true of many human beings that under certain circumstances they find themselves compelled to make choices regarding such stark either-ors. Here are some other examples of such choices, drawn from a variety of fields:

> Either absolute moral standards exist or there is no such thing as morality.
>
> Either a text has a fixed, determinate meaning or it is simply meaningless.
>
> Either something is certain or nothing is even probable.

In each case we are asked to choose between order, unity, and closure, on one side, and disorder, plurality, and unsettledness, on the other. These choices can strike different people differently. Which choices count as profound and urgent will vary from person to person. To some (actually very few), all such choices may seem no more than pretentious nonsense or, at best, things to ponder during idle moments—during downtime. Yet under certain circumstances these radical choices can seem to force themselves on us. They can seem both important and unavoidable. This happens almost inevitably when we step back from the affairs of daily life and engage in that peculiar human activity known as philosophizing.

A decision concerning a choice of this kind involves a two-step process. The first is to accept the choice as being intelligible, forced, and compelling.[3] The second is to decide which option to adopt. The first step is the most important; the second, the choice between options, is relatively less interesting, revealing perhaps nothing more than the temperament of the person making the choice.

Consider the choice between theism and moral nihilism supposedly forced on us by the claim that if there is no God, then everything is (morally) possible. The choice can be given a shallow or a deep reading. The shallow reading comes to this: Unless people are scared skinny by the threat of divine punishment and, beyond this, bribed by the allure of heavenly reward, they cannot be expected to act decently. Santa Claus (read: the Lord returning in awful splendor) is coming to town.

It is also possible to give Dostoyevsky's choice—as we might call it—a deeper reading. Jean-Paul Sartre does so in the following passage:

> The existentialist . . . thinks it very distressing that God does not exist, because all possibility of finding values in a heaven of ideas disappears along with Him; there can no longer be an *a priori* Good, since there is no infinite and perfect consciousness to think it. Nowhere is it written that the Good exists, that we must be honest, that we must not lie; because the fact is we are on a plane where there are only men. Dostoyevsky said, "If God didn't exist, everything would be possible." That is the very starting point of existentialism.[4]

For an atheist such as Sartre, accepting Dostoyevsky's choice leads to a deep sense of the absurdity (emptiness, forlornness) of human existence.

A striking feature of Dostoyevsky's choice, whichever option is taken, is its remoteness from decisions made in ordinary life. This choice is made on a higher plane. Would a theist seriously argue that because we are not permitted to park in front of fire hydrants, there must be a God? Of course not. Reversing things, would a nihilist opponent argue that because there is no God, we *are* permitted to park in front of fire hydrants? This is no better. Here the theists and the nihilists will join forces in ridiculing such talk about fire hydrants as shallow and jejune. They are engaged in a philosophical debate generated by a shared commitment to the centrality of a radical choice between theism and moral nihilism. Given this shared commitment, they will speak with one voice in condemning those who, to their minds, attempt to evade their demand for a fundamental decision. Debates concerning radical choices are carried on in a way that insulates them from the ordinary, workaday world. This is an important fact about them, something that demands close examination.

Because this work is neither about morality nor about religion, reference to Dostoyevsky's choice is intended only as an illustration of a persistent feature of philosophical thinking. This is the tendency for people to reach radically different positions by making opposed choices on what they take to be forced options. Such choices are perhaps more dread-producing when they arise in such areas as religion and morality, but they have a tendency to arise across the entire intellectual landscape, even in its most arid regions. Consider the following claim by the Harvard philosopher C. I. Lewis, a figure as far removed from Dostoyevsky and Sartre as one can imagine. It occurs in his *Analysis of Knowledge and Valuation,* a magisterial work of sober, careful analysis published in 1946.

> If anything is to be probable, then something must be certain.[5]

It yields the last *either-or* on the list given above. We can call it Lewis's choice:

> Either something is certain or nothing is even probable.

In other words, for something to be even probable, some *other* things must be fixed and certain. Convinced, as most of us are, that some beliefs are at the very least probable, Lewis drew the conclusion that at least some things must be certain. He then set himself the task of identifying these underlying certainties and showing how they could provide support for probabilities. Nobody, so far as I know, now thinks that Lewis was successful in this effort, and indeed, there now seems to be a consensus that no such foundationalist strategy in the theory of knowledge has a chance of success.

The intricacies of the debate between foundationalists and their rivals are not, however, my present concern.[6] What interests me is the source of this radical choice between something being certain or, for lack of this, everything being lost. Lewis thinks that this choice is forced on us by the following line of reasoning:

> [In the complete absence of certainty we] will become involved in an indefinite regress of the merely probable— or else . . . go round in a circle—and the probability will fail to be genuine.[7]

The giveaway expression in this passage is the phrase "regress of the *merely* probable." This conjures up the picture of quicksand resting on more quicksand all the way down, thus being incapable of supporting anything. We take it for granted that many things are probably true, indeed, that some things are so highly probable that we just call them true. Relying on this strong commitment of common sense, Lewis's choice yields his doctrine of certainty. However, as always, the game can be played in the reverse direction. The liberated, advanced thinker—the nihilist regarding probabilities—can reject all certainties and then argue that Lewis's choice forces us to acknowledge—despite what the great majority of people might think—that we have no basis for accepting anything with any degree of probability whatsoever.[8] With no ultimately firm ground under our feet, there is no ground under them at all. It seems the only way out of this impasse is to reject the principle I have called Lewis's choice, the either-or principle Lewis shares with his imagined nihilist opponents. Yet under certain circumstances, Lewis's choice, like Dostoyevsky's choice, can seem to force itself on us. It will then seem a mark of intellectual (moral, spiritual) cowardice not to confront it directly.

The point of this work is not to offer guidance in making such choices, but to try to understand how they arise and how, if at all, we can extricate ourselves from them. A central thesis of this work is that such radical choices emerge when reason is given unrestricted employment. A further thesis is that extrication from these choices can be difficult and perhaps, in some cases, never completely successful. These choices can generate what Wittgenstein calls "deep disquietudes."[9] They do so by placing us in the following paradoxical position: The very act of taking such a radical choice seriously walls us off from just those considerations that could extricate us from it. Furthermore, it does not help to tell this to someone wrestling with a radical choice. To him or her, any such suggestion will sound shallow, question-begging, self-sealing, or, as William James would put it, like a "shuffling evasion." This built-in resistance virtually guarantees that no treatment of the anxieties generated by a radical choice is likely to seem fully satisfactory to anyone deeply immersed in it. One possible strategy is to draw a comparison with some other radical choice that the person does not find compelling. Perhaps by exhibiting the underlying similarity between Lewis's choice and Dostoyevsky's choice, we can break the spell of someone's obsession with Lewis's choice; Dostoyevsky, Sartre, and Nietzsche may not be a crowd with which that person wishes to associate. Unfortunately, the opposite can also happen: Our subject may, for the first time, take Dostoyevsky's choice seriously, thus doubling his or her troubles. Contagion spreads.

⚘

Because we will be dealing with difficult issues that crisscross in complex ways, it may help to have a road map for what follows. The first two chapters examine a polarity that takes place at the deepest possible level, the acceptance or rejection of what is often considered the fundamental principle of rational thinking—the law of noncontradiction. This law, which (roughly) tells us that it is not possible for something to both be and not be, or for something to possess a quality yet lack it, can strike one as so fundamental that it seems inconceivable that anyone would reject it. Yet it *has* been rejected, by Heracleitus (at least as some read him), by Ralph Waldo Emerson, by Walt Whitman, and by Friedrich Nietzsche, among others. In postmodernist circles it is considered a mark of naiveté to accept the law of noncontradiction. As we shall see, the dispute between the traditional defenders of the law and its traditional opponents is grounded in a shared misconception of the status of this law—a misconception that yields perhaps the most fundamental radical choice of all. With this shared misconception in place, the dispute is intractable. Unfortunately, the misconception is extremely difficult to dislodge. This story is told in chapter 1.

The second chapter also concerns the law of noncontradiction but has a different tendency. Following Wittgenstein, it actually defends a number of seemingly antirationalist theses, among them that inconsistency does not always render a system useless, that consistency is not always the most important goal of inquiry, and that it might be wholly unreasonable to suppose that human beings will ever be able to attain a view of the world that is both suitably rich and completely consistent. None of this is intended to show that the law of noncontradiction is false. But if correct, it does seem to show that inevitably human beings must live their intellectual lives in the neighborhood of absurdity.

The third chapter, "Pure Reason and Its Illusions," draws on Kant's notion of a dialectical illusion. His *Critique of Pure Reason* begins with these words:

> Human reason has this peculiar fate that in one species of its knowledge it is burdened by questions which, as prescribed by the very nature of reason itself, it is not able to ignore, but which, as transcending all its powers, it is also not able to answer.[10]

When Kant speaks of "one species" of human knowledge, he has in mind traditional a priori metaphysics, that is, an attempt to delineate the fundamental features of the universe employing pure (i.e., nonempirical) methods alone. According to Kant, it is built into our rational faculties to demand such a purely rational account of the universe, yet at the same time our faculties are such that we will never be able to satisfy this demand. For Kant, the only way to extricate ourselves from this bind is to understand and acknowledge the inherent limits of our rational faculties and, having fixed their limits, restrict our intellectual efforts to tasks within our power. But, as Kant saw, the demands of reason are not easily subdued, and if they cannot be satisfied legitimately, reason will bring forth illegitimate offspring and find its satisfaction in them. In this way the human mind generates what Kant calls metaphysical or dialectical illusions—an idea of central importance to this work.

Kant saw that an endless quest for ultimate grounds generates dialectical or metaphysical illusions that, though wholly unfounded, can come to dominate human thinking. Kant saw something else as well: Those who accept the illusory ideals of the metaphysicians but despair of satisfying them will inevitably be led into a radically negative standpoint—skepticism, relativism, perspectivalism, or the like. With respect to skepticism, Kant says, "Skepticism originally arose from metaphysics and its anarchic dialectic."[11] Skepticism, however, is only one of the negative attitudes that thwarted metaphysical yearnings can generate. Various forms of radical or, as we might call it, absolute relativism can arise in the same way, as they have in much postmodern thought. What Kant saw, though this often goes unnoticed, is that those who defend so-called absolutes and those who adopt various forms of absolute relativism *share* a commitment to a rationalist ideal. Those who think that the rationalist ideal can be satisfied swing one way; those who think it cannot, swing the opposite way. Under the sway of the rationalist ideal, no middle ground seems possible, and none is tolerated. Left to itself, reason polarizes into extreme positions, each untenable in its own way, gaining all its strength—again as Kant saw—from the untenability of its opposite.

The fourth chapter concerns skepticism. The notion of a skeptic can be understood in various ways, and the various forms that skepticism can take will be sorted out with some care. Informally, to be skeptical about something is to have doubts concerning it. For example, some economists might be skeptical concerning the continuation of rapid economic growth. As skeptics, they do not deny that rapid economic growth will continue; they simply think that there are no adequate reasons for thinking that it will. In this respect skeptics are modest folks. But people can find the skeptics' modesty unsettling, for their call for suspension of belief can present itself as a challenge to deeply held commitments. The religious skeptic (or agnostic) can seem every bit as threatening to religion as the atheist—indeed, some people find it hard to distinguish the two. But even if the skeptic is not always a welcome guest at a dinner party, a certain measure of skepticism is an essential component of a rational life. A life of reason is a life based on reasons, and this involves the evaluation of reasons, sorting out the good ones from the bad, the adequate from the inadequate, and so on. Without this critical attitude, innovation (for example, in the sciences) would not be possible. It is, or at least should be, one of the primary goals of education to instill healthy skeptical attitudes in students.

There is, however, a risk in developing skeptical or critical attitudes: They can get out of hand. Many of our institutions (political, social, moral, religious) do not fare well when subjected to critical or skeptical scrutiny. Skepticism rarely stands on the side of the establishment, and it is therefore thought dangerous. Here, however, I am not concerned with the embarrassments that a skeptical attitude may cause to those in power. The difficulty that will concern us is that skepticism, though an essential component in rationality, has what seems to be an inherent tendency to become unlimited in its scope, with the result that the edifice of rationality is destroyed. Here skepticism is not, as in the case Kant noted, the result of an unending dialectical battle among contending metaphysical positions; it starts with our common, quite reasonable, standards for judgment. When these standards are given unlimited application, they bring down all knowledge around them. Specifically, when we turn our critical faculties loose on the supposed sources of our knowledge, the fated result is an extreme version of skepticism. I do not know who had this idea first, but David Hume saw it with perfect clarity.

> 'Tis impossible upon any system to defend either our understanding or senses; and we but expose them farther when we endeavour to justify them in that manner.[12]

When we attempt "to defend either our understanding or senses," we find ourselves driven to ask questions of the following kind:

> How can I know that a world exists external to my own mind?
>
> Even if I can know that there is an external world, how can I know what it actually contains?
>
> How can I be rationally assured that the future will resemble the past?
>
> How, even in principle, can the reliability of memory be established?

Much of modern philosophy, that is, philosophy since the seventeenth century, has been an attempt to respond to such skeptical challenges. To my mind, when they are taken on their own terms, no satisfactory response has been found to any one of them. I think that it is highly unlikely that any adequate response will ever be forthcoming. This last remark is not a counsel of despair based on the repeated failure to produce adequate responses to various skeptical challenges. I have come to think that skeptical challenges of the kind just listed wear their unanswerability on their faces—at least, that is how they strike me.

It seems, then, that reason, when its ideals are fully pursued, will inevitably lead to paradox and incoherence (chapter 2), to dialectical illusions of either an absolutist or a relativist flavor (chapter 3), or to a skepticism that closes down the rational enterprise altogether (chapter 4). Given this gloomy account of the "fate of reason," how, it is natural to ask, is daily life protected from its ravages? Well, philosophical jitters do sometimes intrude into daily life— in adolescent alienation, for example. Intellectual laziness and stupidity can play a role in keeping us out of intellectual harm's way. Ignorance, as they say, is bliss. Yet an appeal to stupidity leaves a fundamental question unanswered: Given our precarious status as cognitive agents, how can we account for our progressive intellectual achievements, for example, in the natural sciences? There are, in fact, some advanced thinkers who deny that such progress has occurred. Thomas Kuhn has said some things that suggest this. Various hyper-Kuhnians have made a living dilating on his denial of scientific progress. They provide a paradigm of reason gone haywire and thereby generating strong negative results. They also exhibit the delicious irony of people writing that progress in science is an illusion when the computer beneath their fingertips refutes the very things they are writing on it.

Still, the question remains: How can reason be prevented from disgracing itself? What are the proper precautions needed to prevent this from happening? The closing chapters offer a number of modest suggestions concerning how such disgrace might be avoided. The modesty, the cautiousness, the tentativeness of these suggestions will lead them to be dismissed out of hand by those immersed in dialectical controversies. More generally, these suggestions will be treated with contempt by those committed to the deeply wrongheaded, indeed dangerous standpoint expressed in Revelations 3:15–16:

> I know thy works, that thou art neither cold nor hot: I would thou wert cold or hot. So then because thou art lukewarm, and neither cold nor hot, I will spue thee out of my mouth.

A foolish consistency is the hobgoblin of little minds, adored by little statesmen and philosophers and divines. With consistency a great soul has simply nothing to do.

Ralph Waldo Emerson, "Self Reliance"

Do I contradict myself?
Very well then . . . I contradict myself;
I am large . . . I contain multitudes.

Walt Whitman, "Song of Myself"

The law of contradiction [tells us that] the true world . . . cannot contradict itself, cannot change, cannot become, has no beginning and no end.

This is the greatest error that has ever been committed.

Friedrich Nietzsche, *Will to Power,* #584

Man is a rational animal.

Attributed to Aristotle

CHAPTER ONE

Why Obey
the Laws of Logic?

To the best of my knowledge (and somewhat to my surprise), Aristotle never actually says that man is a rational animal. However, he all but says it. Aristotle held that rationality is the feature that sets human beings apart from all other animals. By this he did not mean that human beings always or even usually think and act in rational ways. He knew better. Like other animals, human beings also possess desires and appetites, and these, if not properly managed by reason, can produce irrational beliefs and irrational ways of acting. For Aristotle, our double nature—namely, that we are rational creatures in some ways and irrational creatures in others—is reflected in the need for two kinds of virtues, intellectual virtues and moral virtues. The intellectual virtues concern the mind's capacity to acquire knowledge or, when knowledge is not possible, at least gain well-founded belief. Moral virtues concern reason's capacity to govern desires and appetites in ways that keep them within their proper limits. To the extent that a person possesses these two kinds of virtues, that person will lead an exemplary human life. An elitist, Aristotle thought that this possibility was fully open to very few and, even for these few, difficult to attain.

Aristotle's account of the intellectual virtues is complex and many-sided, but one of its central ideas is that thought, to be rational, must conform to the laws of logic.[1] To take the primary instance of a violation of a law of logic, it is not rational to hold inconsistent or incompatible beliefs; for example, it is not rational to hold both that God is all-powerful and that God is not all-powerful. To cite a less obvious example, it is not rational to assert that an omnipotent being, a being with unlimited power, could create an object so heavy that it could not be lifted. Making either of these assertions violates one of the fundamental principles of rationality: the *law of contradiction* or, as it is now more reasonably called, the law of *non*contradiction. Traditionally, many philosophers (Aristotle among them) have considered the law of noncontradiction to be the deepest, most fundamental principle of rationality. To abandon that principle is to abandon reason itself and, if Aristotle is right, to abandon the very feature that sets human beings apart from all other animals.

Yet, as the three quotations presented above show, not everyone has treated the law of noncontradiction with respect. Both Emerson and Whitman refuse to be bound by it, and Nietzsche, in his usual hyperbolic fashion, goes so far as to call it "the greatest error that has ever been committed." These three figures are not alone in rejecting the law of noncontradiction. The voice of antirationalism can be found in fragments from ancient pre-Socratic philosophers and reappears two and a half millennia later in the writings of many postmodernists. The status of the law of noncontradiction is the ultimate battleground on which the traditional forces of rationalism and antirationalism have met. An examination of this law, and the battles that have surrounded it, will serve as our starting point, first, because of its fundamental character, and second, because it provides a paradigm of a radical disagreement driven by a shared underlying misunderstanding.

First of all, what is the law of noncontradiction? Stated accurately, if clumsily, it comes to this:

> It is not the case that something is both the case and not the case.[2]

Here some elementary notation will bring out the simple structure of the law of noncontradiction. If we let "~" mean "it is not the case that" and let "&" mean, reasonably enough, "and," then the law of noncontradiction has the following form:

$$\sim(p \ \& \sim p)$$

The claim is this: Take any proposition you please—its subject matter does not matter, nor (as we shall see) does its truth—substitute it in both places for p, and you will always wind up with a proposition that is true. For example, if we let p equal *Lead is heavier than aluminum* (which it is), we get the truth:

1. It is not the case that (both) lead is heavier than aluminum and lead is not heavier than aluminum.

This principle remains true even if we substitute something false for p; for example, if we let p equal *Lead is heavier than uranium* (which it isn't), we get:

2. It is not the case that (both) lead is heavier than uranium and lead is not heavier than uranium.

Because the truth of the proposition we substitute for p makes no difference to the truth of either statement 1 or statement 2, it should be clear that their truth does not depend in any way on the actual weight of these three metals. More generally, it doesn't matter *what* we are talking about when we insert propositions into this pattern. The principle holds as well for daffodils, numbers, and furniture as it does for metals. We thus have a principle that holds with perfect generality. The law of noncontradiction takes any proposition, whatever its subject matter, whether it is true or false, and generates from it a proposition that is always true.

Explaining the law of noncontradiction this way may make it seem altogether trivial. Someone might wonder what all the fuss is about; it is obvious that every statement having the form of the law of noncontradiction will have to be true. That's absolutely right! Noting this triviality, however, has the following important consequence: If you violate the law of noncontradiction by asserting something of the form *It is the case that p and also the case that not p,* you have said something trivially (obviously, boringly, stupidly) false. Looked at this way, ultrairrationalism turns out to be tedious.

If this is correct, as it seems to be, how do we explain the urge found among many historically important figures to reject the law of noncontradiction and find it of fundamental importance to do so? The answer, I think, is that the status of the law of noncontradiction has been persistently misunderstood. Instead of being seen as true but trivial, it is taken to be a powerful and dangerous falsehood. The road to misunderstanding is paved by stating the law of noncontradiction in a more robust ontological form, for example:

> A fact cannot both exist and not exist (or obtain and not obtain).

Or as Aristotle put it:

> The same attribute cannot at the same time belong and not belong to the same subject in the same respect.[3]

This principle, with its reference to facts or attributes, seems to place constraints on the form that reality itself can take. Expressed this way, the law of noncontradiction seems to preclude certain possibilities and to do so in the strongest possible way. This can suggest that the law of noncontradiction, far from being a triviality, is the most fundamental, the most encompassing, and the most constraining law of all. The law of noncontradiction now appears to be a superlaw governing reality in its most fundamental aspects. As Aristotle put it, this principle is true of "being *qua* being."[4]

This way of interpreting the law of noncontradiction is altogether natural and also profoundly mistaken. It is the result of accepting a deeply misleading picture of various laws operating with varying levels of constraint.[5] At the lowest level of constraint, so the story goes, there are human laws or human ordinances. Being commands, these laws can be broken, though it is often considered wrong to do so, and we may be punished if caught. Above these laws in degree of constraint are physical laws, for example, the law of gravity. Unlike human laws, these laws cannot be broken—except, perhaps, if God rescinds them in order to produce a miracle. But even if physical laws cannot be broken, they are still, as it is said, *contingent* laws. The universe is in fact governed by certain physical laws, but it might have been governed by other physical laws or, perhaps, been governed by no physical laws at all. It is this feature of contingency that supposedly sets physical laws below logical laws in stringency: Logical laws govern the world not contingently but, as it is said, *necessarily*.

The thought that the laws of logic—in particular the law of noncontradiction—hold necessarily is sometimes given a quaint turn when it is asserted that even God is bound by the law of noncontradiction. For example, even God could not make a three-sided square. (Calling a triangle a square doesn't do it.) In any case, if we view the law of noncontradiction as a super-(meta)-physical law, then we see why we should not go about contradicting ourselves, for to do so is to be at odds with the universe in its most fundamental (perhaps even God-constraining) aspect.

Perhaps we can now see why people are sometimes inclined to reject the law of noncontradiction: They think that the law of noncontradiction is tied to the picture of laws just sketched, and they refuse to believe that the world conforms to this picture. One reason, perhaps the chief reason, they reject this picture is that they hold that a world governed by the strict, unchanging laws of logic leaves no place for change (creativity, agency, action, progress, fun). For symbolic purposes, I will call those who adopt this position Heracleiteans.[6] Heracleiteans hold that flux, or radical change, rather than unalterable logical structure, is the fundamental characteristic of reality. For Heracleiteans, nothing is stable and unchanging. Granted, certain things may *seem* stable, but down deep all is flux. You cannot step into the same river twice.

Here, then, is a reason for rejecting the law of noncontradiction: The law of noncontradiction, it is thought, is incompatible with real change, but change is real—indeed, it represents the most fundamental aspect of reality. If this is right, then the law of noncontradiction misrepresents the world in its most fundamental aspects.[7] More than two thousand years later Nietzsche, who in various places praises Heracleitus, adopted the Heracleitean view of the world, tying it explicitly to a rejection of the law of noncontradiction.[8] This is the point of the passage cited at the head of this chapter.

> The law of contradiction [tells us that] the true world . . . cannot contradict itself, cannot change, cannot become, has no beginning and no end.

Opposed to the Heracleiteans are those who share this picture of the law of noncontradiction as superconstraining, then, reasoning in the reverse direction, conclude that change is impossible. I will take Parmenides as the symbolic representative of this standpoint.[9] The Parmenideans held that the real, or at least the really real, is rational and, for that reason, one and immutable. This packaging of rationality, reality, unity, and immutability is a persistent feature of Western philosophy. Calling something immutable is still a laudatory thing to say about it. The Judeo-Christian-Islamic God is said to be immutable. (The Greek gods were not immutable, nor are the Hindu gods—that is why they are more fun.) Some still seek immutable truths as the grounds for ethics and forms of government. Unlike the Rolling Stones (paradigmatic Heracleiteans), many people are made uncomfortable by things that "change with every new day."[10] We have not lost our taste for immutability, even in this scientific age. Though cosmic and biological evolution seem undeniable facts, we expect (assume, demand) that the laws underlying these changes must themselves be immutable. A law of nature that changes over time could not, for that very reason, be a real law of nature.[11]

It's interesting to examine the ways in which philosophers attempt to find a middle ground or reconciliation between these extreme Parmenidean and Heracleitean orientations. Partitioning is a favorite device: One part of the universe is deemed Parmenidean, the other Heracleitean. For Plato, the intelligible world—the world of eternal and unchanging forms—is Parmenidean. The world of appearances—the world of flux we inhabit—is Heracleitean. A similar picture appears in Wittgenstein's *Tractatus*, where shifting, lawless, and wholly valueless matters of fact display themselves within an eternal and unchanging logical framework. Hegel attempts to blend these opposing elements into a synthetic whole by declaring:

> Truth is [a] bacchanalian revel, where not a member is sober; and because every member no sooner becomes detached than it *eo ipso* collapses straightway, the revel is just as much a state of transparent unbroken calm.[12]

Through this remarkable maneuver, Hegel adopts the Parmenidean view that the real is rational, while at the same time rejecting the law of noncontradiction.

It is, I think, possible to read the history of philosophy as a series of conflicts and accommodations between the Parmenidean vision and the Heracleitean vision. At the moment, Heracleitus seems to be getting more press than Parmenides—at least among advanced thinkers. Historically, Parmenides has fared better. Fashions change. It is important, however, to see that, despite their deep differences, these primal opponents share a fundamental dogma:

If the law of noncontradiction is true, then change
(real change) is not possible.

Anyone who accepts this conditional will be forced to
choose between the law of noncontradiction and the reality
of change. Opting for the law of noncontradiction, the
Parmenideans reject change. Opting for change, the Heracleiteans reject the law of noncontradiction. Notice, by
the way, that these views share equally in the charm of being
utterly outrageous. Contrary to what Parmenides' student
Zeno says, Achilles can catch the tortoise. Contrary to
Heracleitus, you can step in the same river twice—three or
four times, if you like. Somehow, such plain facts get
demoted to apparent facts, and then dismissed altogether.

My suggestion, then, is that the perennial dispute
between the Heracleiteans and the Parmenideans is driven
by the shared view that the law of noncontradiction is
incompatible with change. How are we to break the spell
of this idea? As noted, this cannot be done by citing plain
facts. Running will not move a Parmenidean; standing still
will not stop a Heracleitean. Instead it has to be shown that
the analogy between physical laws and logical laws (as
superphysical laws) is wholly misguided. This will be our
next topic.

&

Early in the twentieth century, Ludwig Wittgenstein was
worried about the status of laws of logic. He was concerned
with questions of the following kind:

If logical laws are true, what are they true of?

Are there logical facts that would make logical propositions true just as there are physical facts that make physical propositions true?

If so, what would a logical fact be like?

On Christmas Day in 1914, Wittgenstein was visited by an epiphany that he thought showed the way to answer all these questions. He wrote in his notebook:

My fundamental thought is that the logical constants are not proxies [representatives].[13]

To see what Wittgenstein had in mind by this cryptic remark, we can look again at the schematic form of the law of noncontradiction:

It is not the case that it is (both) the case that p and not the case that p.

Or, symbolically:

$\sim(p \,\&\, \sim p)$

This expression provides a pattern or schema for endlessly many propositions, all of which turn out to be true for whatever proposition we substitute for the variable p. Because, as we saw, the content of p can vary endlessly without affecting the truth of the resulting statement, it seems reasonable to suppose that the work of guaranteeing the truth of propositions that conform to this pattern must be done by the two words that do not vary, namely the words "and" and "not." But what do these words *mean*—what do they *stand for?* Wittgenstein's remarkable idea—he called it his "fundamental idea"—was that these words, though meaningful, do not get their meaning by *representing, standing for,* or *referring to* some kind of entity.[14] They do not stand for anything in the world or in the mind or anywhere else. They are nonreferring terms. This is what Wittgenstein had in mind when he said that logical constants—words such as "and" and "not"—are not *representatives.*

The notion that the meaning of a word is the thing or idea that it stands for is deeply ingrained; it strikes many people as simply obvious that a word that does not stand for or represent something must be a dead symbol—a mere mark on paper, hence meaningless.[15] However deeply ingrained or natural this view might seem, Wittgenstein came to think that it was a prejudice—a prejudice that has been the source of endless confusion. In effect, Wittgenstein arrived at this result by setting aside the question "What do words such as 'and' and 'not' stand for?" and asking a better question: "How do these terms contribute to the meaning of the total sentences in which they occur?"

We can start with "not"—negation. We can become utterly baffled if we ask what this word stands for. Does it stand for nothing, nothingness, nonbeing? If so, what sorts of things are they? Does nothing really exist, and if it does exist, is it really nothing? Questions of this kind can sound deep or silly depending on your philosophical mood or temperament. The air clears at once if we set aside the question "What does this word stand for?" and ask quite a different question:

Starting with some proposition p, what happens if we construct its denial using the word "not"?

The negation of a proposition can be constructed in a variety of ways, for example, by putting the word "not" in the appropriate place in front of its main verb. If you want to sound like a logician, you can put the expression "It is not the case that" in front of the whole sentence. There are other ways of negating a sentence as well, but however negation is achieved, we get the following result:

If a proposition is true, then the proposition that results from negating it is false, and if a proposition is false, then the proposition that results from negating it is true.

Wittgenstein captured this idea by introducing what came to be known as a truth-table definition of negation. Using the symbol for negation introduced earlier, the truth-table definition looks like this:

p	$\sim p$
T	F
F	T

It is important to see that nothing esoteric (or sly) is going on here. The left-hand column indicates the two truth-values that a proposition can have: It can be true or it can be false. The second column indicates what happens when a proposition is negated; its truth-value is reversed. Negation, we might say, is a truth-value flip-flopper.

If we now ask what gives negation the power to reverse truth-values in this way, Wittgenstein says (in effect) that the question is misconceived. For him, the meaning of the word "not" consists in its capacity to reverse truth-values. This is its job—hence its meaning—in our language.[16] It took the insight of a genius to see that the definition of negation should take this form, for this truth-table definition looks nothing like the definitions we commonly offer for nouns, verbs, and so on. This difference in form reflects the special role that logical words play in our language. Recognizing the appropriateness of using truth tables to define certain logical terms represented a fundamental advance in logic. It was also an important first step in breaking the spell of an overly simple view of the way language functions.[17]

Having given a truth-table definition of negation, we can turn next to conjunction. A conjunction of two propositions is true just in case both of the conjoined propositions are true; otherwise it is false. Thus the truth-table definition of conjunction looks like this:

p	q	$p \mathbin{\&} q$
T	T	T
T	F	F
F	T	F
F	F	F

Here the first two columns of the truth table show all the possible combinations of truth-values for p and q; the third column shows the truth-value of the conjunction for each combination. Reflecting the underlying idea of conjunction, only the first row is marked true; the other rows are marked false. Again, the novelty of this definition does not lie in the particular values we have assigned to conjunction in this truth table—that should seem trivial. The importance lies in taking this truth table as a *definition* of conjunction.

With truth-table definitions of both negation and conjunction in hand, we are now in a position to look at the law of noncontradiction with new (let's hope scale-free) eyes. Specifically, we are now in a position to address the question "What makes the law of noncontradiction true?" or "In virtue of what is it true?" The appropriate truth table for the law of noncontradiction looks like this:

A	B	C	D
p	$\sim p$	$p \mathbin{\&} \sim p$	$\sim(p \mathbin{\&} \sim p)$
T	F	F	T
F	T	F	T

Again, nothing esoteric is going on. Moving through three stages, we have constructed a truth table for the law of noncontradiction. Column A gives the two possible truth-values for p (T and F). In column B we have constructed $\sim p$ by reversing the truth-values of p. In column C we have conjoined p and $\sim p$. Given the truth-table definition of conjunction, we know that this conjunction has to be false no matter what truth-value is assigned to p. (Thus, in column C, we have constructed the pattern for an explicit self-contradiction.) In column D we have simply negated the formula in column C, thereby producing the pattern for the law of noncontradiction. Given the truth table for negation, the result is that the truth-values under column C are reversed for column D—where originally they were all false, they are now all true.

We now have something quite simple to say to the Heracleitean who finds nothing wrong in affirming an explicit contradiction. As column C indicates, whatever the subject matter of the remark, the Heracleitean must be saying something false. To think otherwise is to suffer from a curious form of linguistic ignorance concerning the words "not" and "and." Willard Quine put it this way: "[To] affirm a compound of the form '*p* and not *p*' is just to have mislearned one or both [of these] particles."[18] But even if this embarrasses the Heracleitean, it gives little aid or comfort to the Parmenidean, for now the law of noncontradiction (represented in column D) emerges as a barren tautology—a purely empty or formal truth. To vary one of Wittgenstein's examples, to be told that it is not the case that it is both raining and not raining is not to be told anything about the weather—or about anything else.

If this account is correct, then the picture of the law of noncontradiction as a superlaw of reality has been undermined. The law of noncontradiction, rather than placing ultimate constraints on reality, places *no* constraints on reality at all. Furthermore, we now see that the view shared by the Heracleiteans and the Parmenideans, that *change is incompat-*

ible with the law of noncontradiction, rests on a misunderstanding. The Heracleitean is wrong in thinking that we must deny the law of noncontradiction in order to affirm the existence of change. The Parmenidean is wrong in thinking that we must deny the existence of change in order to preserve the law of noncontradiction.

They are both wrong, and wrong for the same reason. They share the view that change and the law of noncontradiction are incompatible when, in fact, the law of noncontradiction has no bearing on the possibility of change one way or the other.

&

It's time to slow down, for it may now seem that we have managed to do something that Aristotle (in agreement with a great many other philosophers) thought could not be done, namely, provide a proof or demonstration of the law of noncontradiction. Because the law of noncontradiction lies at the basis of all demonstration, it was not, Aristotle thought, capable of proof or demonstration.[19] I think Aristotle is fundamentally right in this regard, and nothing I have said is intended to deny this. Though truth-table definitions may help us understand the status of the law of noncontradiction, they cannot be used to prove it. The difficulty is this: In constructing these truth-table definitions, we seem to be taking the law of noncontradiction (or something close to it) for granted. To see the problem, we can look again at the truth table for negation:

p	$\sim p$
T	F
F	T

Here, without a word of justification or explanation, we have simply taken it for granted that a proposition can be true and that a proposition can be false, but we have not considered the possibility that it might be *both* true and false. That is, we have not taken into consideration a truth table of the following kind:

p	$\sim p$
T	F
F	T
	T-F ?

It may seem obvious that this third row does not represent a genuine possibility, but it appears that any attempt to establish this impossibility will itself rely on the law of noncontradiction, the very thing we are trying to prove. So it seems that any attempt to prove the law of noncontradiction using truth-table definitions will presuppose the law of noncontradiction and, in that sense, be circular.

Aristotle knew nothing of modern truth-table definitions. His argument rested on the general claim that the law of noncontradiction is a fundamental assumption of *all* demonstration, and therefore cannot be justified by demonstration in a way that is not question-begging. The impossibility of using truth tables to prove the law of noncontradiction is simply a clear illustration of Aristotle's general point. This result may seem unsettling, for it may now appear that we have to accept the law of noncontradiction simply as a matter of faith. If so, it is not clear how we are to deal with people (Emerson, Whitman, Nietzsche, et al.) who place their faith elsewhere.

Here, however, Aristotle comes to our rescue. Though he denies the possibility of giving a positive proof or demonstration of the law of noncontradiction, he suggests that the law of noncontradiction could be demonstrated "negatively."[20] This negative mode of demonstration proceeds as follows: Confronted with someone who wishes to reject the law of noncontradiction, we simply wait for that person either to assert or to deny something, and then ask whether it makes any difference whether we interpret the remark as an assertion or a denial. If the person rejects the law of noncontradiction, it is hard to see why it should make a difference one way or another. In effect, a person who rejects the law of noncontradiction is granting us the following permission:

> In interpreting what I say, you may add the phrase "It is not the case that" to the front of any sentence I utter. Do this as you please, for it will in no way alter the significance of my discourse.

One who denies the law of noncontradiction might also announce the following hermeneutical principle that he or she uses in interpreting the utterances of others:

> In interpreting the discourse of others, I randomly put
> the phrase "It is not the case that" at the front of sentences
> I am interpreting. Given the kind of interpretation I am
> engaged in, this in no way affects its significance.

In fact, if we accept the principle of standard logic that
everything follows from a contradiction, we get the following remarkable principle of interpretation:

> In interpreting discourse, you may, as I do, substitute
> any sentence for any other sentence without affecting
> the significance of what is being said.[21]

If this isn't the outer reaches of anything goes, it is certainly
very close. A person who persistently employed language
in this way would be deemed mad—in the clinical sense of
that term.

Has anyone ever accepted such principles of interpretation? Well, some mystics sometimes seem to. Some
mystics seem to have held that the attributes of God so
transcend human comprehension that it is a matter of
indifference whether we apply humanly intelligible properties to him/her/it or not. But even mystics usually have
the good sense to restrict these views to the mystical—
which, they think, transcends all forms of discourse. Most
people, even those who espouse extreme postmodern
views, actually reject these wild principles of interpretation
(at least when not presenting papers at conferences).

I can illustrate this last point anecdotally. I once found
myself in a room of advanced thinkers where I was the sole

person with a good word to say about the law of noncontradiction. As a result, I was subjected to a great deal of ridicule and abuse. I tried to explain to the audience members—as I have tried to explain here—that in rejecting the law of noncontradiction, they were, in all likelihood, not rejecting the principle itself but instead rejecting a false picture that they mistakenly associated with it. They would have none of this—hell-bent on performing a slam-dunk against logophallocentric Western rationalism, they would accept no such temporizing compromise. In exasperation I finally employed what is called an impolite ad hominem. I asked whether the organizers of the conference were applying for future funding from the National Endowment for the Humanities. When some indicated that they were, I asked if it would make any difference to them whether the answer to their request was no rather than yes, and if so, why? Not surprisingly, this produced a reaction of rage.

What is the point of all this? After all, people do not actually adopt the wild principles of interpretation I have laid out, even if they sometimes speak in ways that suggest they do. If they don't really adopt them, we want to know why not. If we accept the law of noncontradiction, we then have straightforward reasons for rejecting these wild principles of interpretation. On the other hand, if we reject the law of noncontradiction—that is, really reject it, not just pretend to reject it—it is hard to think of any reason for not engaging in anything-goes interpretations in this perfectly mad way. As Aristotle saw, this does not amount to a proof of the law of noncontradiction. It merely shows that people who reject the law of noncontradiction obliterate any significant differ-

ence between asserting something and denying it. In rejecting the law of noncontradiction, they deprive themselves of
the significant use of these speech acts.[22] Sincere, they are
self-silencers. This is Aristotle's "negative demonstration" of
the law of noncontradiction in a somewhat modern guise.
None of this will move anyone who genuinely opts either
for silence or for madness. Because I opt for neither, I find
Aristotle's negative demonstration of the law of noncontradiction entirely persuasive.[23]

In accepting Aristotle's negative demonstration of the
law of noncontradiction, I still disagree with him on a
fundamental matter: his interpretation of this law as a
superlaw governing being qua being. Thus my treatment
of the problem of change is different from that of Aristotle.
Aristotle held, quite correctly, that the law of noncontradiction is compatible with change. He thought that those
who were inclined to think otherwise were captives of a
faulty conception of change. My diagnosis is different: I
hold that those who think that the law of noncontradiction
is incompatible with change suffer from a faulty conception
of the law of noncontradiction. This faulty conception was
shared by all parties in the ancient debate concerning
change—by the Parmenideans, by the Heracleiteans, and
by Aristotle as well. I have suggested that the same error
appears in the writings of Nietzsche. It reappeared in the
twentieth century and will certainly survive through the
twenty-first. This misunderstanding of the status of the law
of noncontradiction has been a deep and perennially
seductive error.[24]

It seems, then, that we have ended on a cheery note. Anxieties about the law of noncontradiction infringing on spontaneity are misguided. When people have worried about this, they should not have worried. Yet, as we shall see in the next chapter, there are problems—deep problems—concerning consistency that do not rest on a misunderstanding of the law of noncontradiction. These are problems generated by the persistent occurrence of paradoxes, dilemmas, and other forms of incoherence. This will be our next topic.

We lay down rules, a technique, for a game, and then when we follow the rules, things do not turn out as we had assumed. . . . We are therefore entangled in our own rules.

This entanglement in our rules is what we want to understand (i.e. get a clear view of) . . . .

In those cases things turn out otherwise than we had meant, foreseen. That is just what we say when, for example, a contradiction appears: "I didn't mean it like that."

The civil status of a contradiction, or its status in civil life: there is the philosophical problem.

Ludwig Wittgenstein,
Philosophical Investigations, #125

CHAPTER TWO

Dilemmas and Paradoxes

In the previous chapter I struck some blows for sanity by arguing that it is an error—indeed, a foolish error—to deny the law of noncontradiction. In this chapter what I say may suggest that I have switched sides. Seemingly becoming more tolerant of contradictions, I will argue that there is no reason to suppose that the rules governing our cognitive activities either do or must form consistent systems. More strongly, I will argue that it is evident that the rules governing many human institutions are *not* consistent. Acknowledging this fact (if it is a fact) does not, by itself, force us to modify a strong commitment to consistency. Discovering an inconsistency may simply set us the task of remedying matters by finding some way of modifying our rules so that the inconsistency no longer arises. Two further commitments, however, may suggest that I have crossed the line into antirationalism. I will argue, I believe following Wittgenstein, that in practice it is often quite reasonable to employ systems of rules with no guarantee that they are consistent. This is a common situation: We employ systems of rules without being able to establish their consistency, perhaps without having any idea of how one might go about doing so. More radically, again following Wittgenstein, I hold that it is sometimes legitimate to continue to use a system of rules even *after* its inconsistency has been recognized. Inconsistency in a system of rules is sometimes debilitating, but not always. Sometimes the best available strategy is to learn to live with inconsistency in, as we might say, a discriminating and civilized manner.

It is important to recognize that in the previous paragraphs I have switched from talking about *propositions* (assertions, statements, and the like) to talking about *rules*. This change is of fundamental importance and should be explained. Although the difference between rules and propositions is complicated and hard to get right, roughly, propositions state how things are, rules guide conduct. Games (for example, board games and card games) provide a natural example of how rules function. In chess we are told that, with certain restrictions, the bishop may move along the diagonal it occupies. It may not move in any other way. The rules governing its moves are *essential* to a piece's being a bishop. A chess piece will also possess nonessential features. The material it is made of is not an essential feature of a bishop; neither is its shape. It is convenient, of course, to have a conventional shape for the bishop, but chess can be played using pieces of paper with the words "bishop," "king," "pawn" written on them. Chess has been played using various sizes of salt and pepper shakers. Chess could even be played on a giant grid with different makes of automobiles representing various pieces. A BMW will be a bishop—and not simply represent one—if it is used in a game of chess with its moves on the grid constrained by the rules appropriate for a bishop.[1]

One of Wittgenstein's leading ideas was this: Just as pieces in a game such as chess are defined by the rules that govern their moves, the meanings of words are similarly defined by the rules that govern their employment.[2] In *Philosophical Investigations,* Wittgenstein tells us, "For a *large* class of cases—though not for all—in which we employ the word 'meaning' it can be defined thus: the meaning of a word is its use in the language."[3] To understand the meaning of a word is to understand (at least implicitly) the rules that govern its use. We encountered a version of this idea in the previous chapter, where we saw that the word "and" could be defined as a connective between sentences that yields a true sentence just in case both sentences it connects are true, and yields a false sentence otherwise. To understand this is to understand how the word "and" is used and therefore to understand its meaning.

In the latter half of his philosophical career Wittgenstein extended this use conception of meaning across the board, producing what many have thought to be a revolution in philosophy.[4] If we want to understand the meaning of some problematic terms, say, numerals, he tells us to examine the *language games* in which they are employed—perhaps even inventing primitive language games where the use of such terms and the rules governing them become transparent. What we discover when we adopt this approach is that words are used in a wide variety of different kinds of language games and therefore possess meanings in a wide variety of different ways. Philosophical confusion arises when we attempt to reduce this large, sprawling plurality of ways that words can have meaning to one or a few simple paradigms. The most common mistake, and the most philosophically pernicious, is to assume that all words (or at least all cognitively significant words) get their meaning by *standing for* or *representing* objects or properties of objects. The doctrine that meaning equals use was intended to break the spell of this primitive way of understanding how our language functions.

For Wittgenstein, the comparison between the rules that govern language and the rules that govern games sheds light on the nature of language, but he also saw that this comparison has hazards of its own. In particular, he thought that the comparison with games, if misunderstood, could lead us to embrace an overly intellectualized or idealized view of the way that the rules governing our use of language actually work. The rules governing chess, as well as the rules governing many logical and mathematical systems, are rigorous and consistent. This can tempt us to think that the rules governing common uses of language must be similarly strict and consistent—or, at the very least, that it should be our goal to attain such strictness and consistency. Wittgenstein rejects both parts of this claim. I agree with him, for it seems clear to me that many of the systems of rules we follow are in fact inconsistent, and beyond this, it seems inevitable that, in some cases at least, we have no course other than to learn how to live with this inconsistency.

I can illustrate the kind of inconsistency I have in mind and what living with inconsistency amounts to by adapting an example taken from Wittgenstein's *Remarks on the Foundations of Mathematics*. The fundamental idea is Wittgenstein's, the embellishments my own.[5] Imagine a board game as complicated and challenging as chess. It has been played for centuries; tournaments are held, world champions are crowned, books and magazines are published concerning it. The ability to excel at this game is taken as a mark of high intelligence. We will call the game Ludwig. One day two novices playing foolishly (though making legal moves) stumble into a position where two of the rules of the game come into conflict. The conflict arises in the following way. Ludwig, like other games, has rules of various kinds. It has rules specifying the ways that pieces are permitted to move. It also has rules indicating that, under certain circumstances, a move is mandatory—as in checkers you have to jump a piece if you are able to jump a piece.[6] It also has rules that, under certain circumstances, forbid making moves that are otherwise legal—as in chess one is not allowed to expose one's king to check. Our novices somehow work their way into a position where a particular move is both mandated and forbidden, thus leaving no legal way to proceed. The game gets "hung up," as computer programs sometimes do. Because this possibility exists, we can say that Ludwig is inconsistent in the following sense:

A series of legal moves can lead to a situation where a further move is both mandated and forbidden.[7] We might say that the system of rules governing Ludwig is, in this sense, dilemma-prone. Finally, we can suppose that this feature of the rules—its dilemma-proneness—has gone undetected for centuries because the moves that lead to it, though legal, are wholly unmotivated. Nobody who understands the *point* of the game Ludwig would make the moves leading to this situation.

Given that Ludwig is dilemma-prone, what are we to say about its status as a game? Given that Ludwig is inconsistent in the sense of being dilemma-prone, are we forced to say that it really isn't a game at all? And if we say it isn't a game, are we further forced to say that those who previously played Ludwig weren't *really* playing a game, even though they mistakenly thought they were? At the very least, once the dilemma-proneness of Ludwig is discovered, don't the rules have to be amended so that this impasse can no longer arise in legal play? Wittgenstein's answer to all these questions—and I follow him in this—would be no.[8]

As described, the conflict in rules will never appear in *serious* play. Indeed, it took a remarkable sequence of stupid moves to generate it. (It is like a land mine planted where no one will step on it—say, at the bottom of a well.) Given this, it seems wholly arbitrary to say that those who played the game before the incoherence was discovered were not really playing a game at all and were deluded in thinking otherwise. Beyond this, even after the inconsistency is discovered, it is not obvious that means must be found to remove it before Ludwig can legitimately be played again.

Various responses are possible. If the rules are easily fixed, then, perhaps for the sake of elegance, the rules might be changed. On the other hand, because Ludwig's dilemma-proneness in no way affects serious play, people may decide to ignore it. Getting rid of the inconsistency might not be worth the trouble of printing new rulebooks. It could also turn out—and this is more interesting—that revising the rules to block the dilemma might be difficult to do in a satisfactory way. Blocking the dilemma could make the game overly complicated, perhaps so complicated that people could no longer play it in an effective way. Eliminating the potential conflict in rules could also have the reverse effect of making the game trivially simple and thus uninteresting to play. Perhaps, for example, with the necessary rule changes, it becomes obvious that whoever moves first always wins. This, then, is the first thesis I wish to maintain: The presence of an inconsistency in the rules that govern a game need not destroy the game; indeed, avoiding inconsistency could make the game unplayable or uninteresting. In some circumstances, we can live, and live happily, in the neighborhood of inconsistency. I will say that a game and, by extension, any system of rules is Ludwigean if, like Ludwig, it is dilemma-prone yet perfectly playable when moves are made in a serious, purposive manner.

Having introduced the idea of a system of rules being dilemma-prone but still serviceable because Ludwigean, we can now turn to human institutions of importance and ask whether they sometimes exhibit Ludwigean features as well. Human behavior is pervasively rule-governed. The behavior of other animals seems rule-governed as well, sometimes in quite complicated ways. However, a distinctive feature of human beings is that over a wide range of cases our behavior has an essential linguistic component.[9] There are things that only language users can do because using language is essential to doing them. (Only language users can buy stock options or engage in cultural criticism.) Furthermore, using language is itself a rule-governed activity. As noted, Wittgenstein gave prominence to these ideas by speaking of language games. According to him, when we employ a language, we enter into a wide range of language games governed by a variety of rules, more or less complex, more or less strict. Our first question is this: Given that the use of language can profitably be viewed as playing various language games, are some of these language games—in particular, some of the important ones—dilemma-prone? Second, granting that some of these language games are dilemma-prone, can they, like Ludwig, still be serviceable or usable? Are they, that is, Ludwigean? My general answer is that many fundamental human institutions are (or are at best) Ludwigean.

To see that our language in its most general features is dilemma-prone, we need only consider the rules that govern sentence construction. They allow the formulation of expressions of the following kind:

(1) The sentence that George just uttered is false.

This is a perfectly ordinary remark that seems unproblematic—it is a way of denying what George just said and will be true just in case what George just said was false. What, however, are we to make of the following claim?

(2) This very sentence [i.e., sentence 2] is false.

This sentence, though grammatically well constructed, produces the following paradoxical result: If it is true, then it is false, and if it is false, then it is true. Notice: If it is true, then, because what it says of itself is that it is false, it must be false; and if it is false, then, because what it says of itself is that it is false, it must be true. So it is true if and only if it is false—and that is paradoxical. This is one example of a large family of paradoxes commonly called liar paradoxes. Sentences that generate liar paradoxes are sometimes called liar sentences.

The liar paradox had its origins in the ancient world. It was one of seven puzzles found on a list compiled by a somewhat mysterious figure, Eubulides of Miletus.[10] There is no evidence indicating what Eubulides thought about these puzzles—whether, for him, they presented serious philosophical challenges or only idle curiosities. Over the centuries, liar paradoxes have been presented in various forms. Here is another example: Plato says, "What Aristotle says is true." Aristotle says, "What Plato says is false." In this case, what Plato says is true if and only if what he says is false. Not only that; Aristotle is in precisely the same pickle. Ancient and medieval logicians were fond of examples of this kind and rang endless changes on them. It was, however, in the twentieth century that the liar paradox put in its most dramatic appearance. A variant of this paradox lies at the heart of what some take to be the most profound discovery in the foundations of mathematics, Gödel's incompleteness theorem.[11]

What are we to say about the liar paradox? Many people are familiar with this paradox (in one of its forms), but do not let it bother them. They may be amused by it, perhaps bored by it, but in any case, they do not think they have to deal with it before again calling certain sentences true and others false. In contrast to this practical approach, where the liar paradox is not scratched because it does not produce a serious itch, the standard reaction among philosophers and logicians is to try to do something about it because it seems to present a serious threat to rationality in general.

Responses to this paradox fall into two broad categories, those that attempt to *dissolve* it (that is, show that it is not really a paradox) and those that attempt to find ways of *avoiding* it (that is, try to find ways of revising our rules so that the paradox no longer arises). Those who adopt the first approach and attempt to dissolve the liar paradox have rough going, for sentence 2 seems paradoxical on its face. The paradox simply shows what happens when we combine the notion of falsehood with self-reference in a particular way. Nothing in our language as we actually use it stands in the way of formulating such sentences. Alfred Tarski speaks of the universality of our language, namely, its lack of restrictions on what we may speak about. We can speak about anything we please, including our language itself. We can also formulate the denial of anything we please. This permissiveness allows the formation of sentence 2, along with the paradox that flows from it.[12] If this is right, then our language is dilemma-prone just as the imagined game of Ludwig is dilemma-prone.

There is, however, one somewhat plausible way of avoiding the paradoxical character of liar sentence 2. It was suggested by Wittgenstein:

"The Cretan Liar." He might have written "This proposition is false" instead of "I am lying." The answer would be: "Very well, but which proposition do you mean?"—"Well, *this* proposition."—"I understand, but which is the proposition mentioned in *it*?"— *"This* one."—"Good, and which proposition does *it* refer to?" and so on. Thus he would be unable to explain what he means until he passes to a complete proposition.[13]

This avoids generating a contradiction by using what we might call the method of delayed evaluation. Before we can evaluate a proposition as being either true or false, we must first identify the proposition to be evaluated. Thus, if the reader is told that the third sentence in this chapter is true, she must first go back and look at that sentence before she can decide whether the evaluation is correct or not. According to Wittgenstein, a sentence such as 2 sends us off on an endless, looping search for the proposition to be evaluated. It goes something like this:

> Proposition 2 tells us that a certain proposition, i.e., proposition 2, is false, so let's see what proposition 2 says.
>
> Well, proposition 2 tells us that a certain proposition, i.e., proposition 2, is false, so let's see what proposition 2 says.
>
> Well, proposition 2 tells us that a certain proposition, i.e., proposition 2, is false, so let's see what proposition 2 says.
>
> And so on forever.

Because we are never in a position to say whether proposition 2 is either true or false, we never get into a position where the liar paradox emerges.

I confess to finding this treatment of the liar paradox somewhat persuasive, but it is important to see that it simply replaces one conceptual disaster with another. Instead of falling into paradox, we are sent off into infinite looping, and that is just as bad. To see this, we can go back to the dilemma that arose in the game of Ludwig and imagine someone trying to fix it using a parallel device. Along with the pieces that are used in setting up the game, players are each given a duplicate set of pieces. When a dilemma arises, they are instructed to remove the offending piece from the board and replace it with a duplicate. That, however, simply reinstates the dilemma, so the piece must be exchanged again for its duplicate— and so on forever. We can call this new game Ludwig 2. Ludwig 2 does avoid the dilemma, because when one arises, the player is forced to exchange pieces endlessly and thus is never in a position to make any move, either legal or illegal. The original Ludwig, encountering a dilemma, is like a computer program that crashes, showing a picture of a bomb on the screen, whereas Ludwig 2 is like a computer that goes into an unending loop. They are both conceptual disasters, bad things that can happen when we give our rules universal or unrestricted application. For those who think that the infinite loop is somehow less disastrous than an outright paradox, I can only quote Wittgenstein (perhaps against himself— I am not sure):

Contradiction. Why just this *one* bogy? That is surely very suspicious.[14]

In contrast to those who attempt to dissolve or dismiss the liar paradox, others grant that the paradox is genuine and then set themselves the task of *revising* the rules of our language in a way that avoids paradox. Not just any solution will do. If our only goal is to solve the paradox, that is easy enough—we simply weaken our language in a way that makes it impossible to construct liar sentences. We might, for example, limit our communication to a single sentence, say, $2 + 2 = 4$. That gets consistency on the cheap but is not the sort of solution that anyone is looking for. We want a solution that preserves most of the strength of our current language while at the same time avoiding paradox. Furthermore, the adjustments we make in the rules governing our language ought to make sense to us. If the liar paradox could be avoided by making adjustments to our language that are intuitively plausible, we could then legitimately speak of *solving* the liar paradox rather than merely *ducking* it by constructing another language in which it does not arise. As far as I can see, no proposed solution to the liar paradox meets this standard of intuitive plausibility. The proposed solutions invariably either involve ad hoc devices that have no inherent plausibility, or ask us to give up things that are themselves inherently plausible.

I will not try to survey such attempted solutions here. There are a great many, and some are fiercely technical. Here I will only comment briefly on one of the standard strategies. Because allowing a sentence to refer to itself—

either directly or through intermediary sentences—is what seems to be causing the trouble, the obvious solution is not to let sentences do that. One way to accomplish this—I will ignore technical details—is to assign an index number to all sentences; for example, "The cat is on the mat" could become "The cat is on the mat.$_7$" We introduce the rule that one sentence can refer to another only if the former has a higher index number than the latter. Given this restriction, no sentence can refer to itself, either directly or indirectly through intermediate sentences. Because a paradox will break out anew if we stop numbering sentences at some level, it will be necessary to have an infinite hierarchy of indexed sentences, but, with that, the liar paradox will be avoided.

Again, it will prove helpful to see what happens if we apply a parallel strategy to our original version of Ludwig. We can produce a new game, Ludwig 3, in the following way. Instead of giving each player a single duplicate set of pieces, as in Ludwig 2, we will give each player endlessly many duplicate sets of pieces. (We will assume that each set of pieces is numbered from 1 on up.) Now when the dilemma appears, the offending piece is removed and is replaced by a duplicate from the first set of duplicates. This reinstates the dilemma, so a further duplicate is substituted from the second set of duplicates. And so on, and so on. As with Ludwig 2, the player of Ludwig 3 is never in a position where he can make a move, for there is always something else he has to do first. In Ludwig 3, one does not go into an endless loop, as happened in Ludwig 2; instead, one is faced with the task of climbing an endlessly high ladder. It may seem that Ludwig 2 has certain practical advantages over Ludwig 3—it demands many fewer pieces. We will, however, set aside this practical matter by assuming that God—a being capable of creating endlessly many pieces— is playing the game. The point I wish to make is that these two ways of avoiding the dilemma in Ludwig seem every bit as unsatisfactory as the dilemma itself.

To draw the moral of this story with respect to the liar paradox, there are ways of understanding or reforming our language so that the liar paradox does not occur in it, but at least in the two cases examined, the cure, though no worse than the disease, seems as bad. If we start out with an obsession with avoiding paradox, then being forced into endless looping or infinite ascent may be taken as something we have to live with. If, however, our obsessions are different and we abhor infinite tasks, then acceptance of the occasional paradox may seem a small price to pay.

The counterintuitive character of attempts to solve the liar paradox exhibits its conceptual depth. It has proven extraordinarily resistant to an adequate treatment. But even if the liar paradox is a deep paradox, this does not mean that we stand under the necessity of doing something about it before we can legitimately make use of our paradox-prone language. Our situation precisely parallels that of *serious* players of the game Ludwig. Most people are oblivious to the liar paradox, but this puts them in no jeopardy because their serious activities never take them into the region where liar sentences lurk. Those who are aware of the liar paradox at least know where the dangers lie and, with good sense, can keep themselves out of harm's way.[15]

Dilemma-proneness goes beyond the paradoxes found in mathematics and logic; indeed, it seems to be a pervasive feature of the systems of rules that make up our most fundamental human institutions, including the institutions of morality and law. In logic and mathematics, paradoxes can be given a clear statement and rigorously deduced from seemingly acceptable sets of axioms. This is not usually possible for moral and legal systems, if for no reason other than that they do not admit of rigorous formulation. However, if sufficient pressure is put on such systems of rules—especially if we confront them with hard or exotic cases—they often yield conflicting or incoherent results.

A potential for moral dilemmas and legal dilemmas is, I believe, an inherent feature of all rich and complex moral and legal systems.[16] To the extent that these systems are serviceable despite their dilemma-proneness, they can be called Ludwigean. There is, however, an important difference between the game of Ludwig and the game of life. In Ludwig, those who play the game seriously and intelligently do not encounter the paradox latent in the rules. Under serious play, it is as if the dilemma were not there, for serious players never go into the region where the dilemma threatens. The game of life is not always this accommodating, for sometimes dilemmas force themselves on us in our serious pursuits of living.

Concentrating for the moment on systems of morality, I suggest that the reason they are dilemma-prone is that they embody a plurality of moral principles or a plurality of forms of moral consciousness that normally coincide but sometimes conflict. Various ethical theories reflect these various principles—though often in exaggerated, one-sided ways. For example, given a choice between two lines of action, where one brings more benefits than the other, it seems obvious—something hardly worth discussing—that we should choose the more, rather than the less, beneficial line of action. There are many contexts in which decisions are pretty much automatically decided on just these grounds. Examples easily come to mind. By dwelling on examples of this kind, one can be drawn in the direction of what is called a *consequentialist* view in ethics. On this approach, the correctness of an action is always judged by the goodness and badness of the consequences that it is likely to produce. That is the broad idea; how it is worked out in detail admits of endless variation.

It can also seem obvious that it is wrong to harm one person to benefit another if the person harmed has not consented to the harm or in no way deserves it. It is not right to take from Peter to pay Paul unless Peter consents to the transfer or is under some obligation to accept it. By dwelling on clear cases of this kind, one can be drawn to a rights-and-duties ethics—called in the trade deontological theories.

We can imagine a world where consequentialist considerations and deontological considerations always coincide in the actions they call for and prohibit. Indeed, in large measure, this is *our* world, the very one we inhabit, for over a wide range of cases the moral demands from these two perspectives coincide. Often enough, taking from Peter to pay Paul does not yield the most beneficial outcome. Yet sometimes it does, and in such circumstances consequentialist and deontological considerations may clash. William James asks us to consider a case in which "millions [could be made] permanently happy on the one simple condition that a certain lost soul on the far-off edge of things should lead a life of lonely torture." James speaks of a "specific and independent sort of emotion" that would make us "feel, even though an impulse arose within us to clutch at the happiness so offered, how hideous a thing would be its enjoyment when deliberately accepted as the fruit of such a bargain."[17] If James is correct, the violation of a single person's rights carries with it a moral repugnance that overrides this massive gain in happiness for the millions (now billions) who will benefit from this bargain. Though the heavens fall, there are certain things we should never do. But is James right? If we focus on the unmerited suffering of the single victim—let it really sink in—we will, I think, tend to react as James reacts. If, instead, we immerse ourselves in the vast misery that exists in the world, then our inclinations may be just the reverse. We should feel sympathy for the poor soul who suffers for our benefit, and we also have a reasonable complaint against the powerful being offering this bargain, who, for no apparent reason, is a moral underachiever. Nevertheless, to be realistic, it may strike us as moral cowardice, generated perhaps by an obsessive desire for clean hands, to reject an offer that would produce so much good for a proportionately insignificant amount of evil.

James's example is a fantasy, but it has genuine counterparts in the world in which we live. Should a terrorist be tortured in an effort to force him to reveal where he has planted an atomic weapon? Perhaps it can be argued that torture under such circumstances, though regrettable, is morally permitted because the terrorist is himself a wrong-doer. Suppose, however, that the terrorist stands up to the torture and reveals nothing. In this case, is it morally permissible to torture one of his innocent children before his eyes in an effort to get the terrorist to reveal his secret? This seems morally impermissible—until, perhaps, we reflect on the large number of innocent children who will be killed and maimed if the terrorist cannot be made to reveal where the bomb is planted. Faced with a radical choice of this kind, there is a strong (and understandable) temptation to duck it. People sometimes say things of the following kind: "It is, of course, morally wrong to torture an innocent child, but sometimes we have no other choice but to act immorally." This might just mean that on certain occasions we have to act in ways that in normal circumstances would be immoral. This, however, is merely a roundabout way of adopting the consequentialist solution to this problem while at the same time throwing a sop to one's deontological conscience.[18]

Who is right? In this case, is it morally right or is it morally wrong to torture the innocent child? My inclination is to say that there is no reason to suppose that there is a definitive answer to this question. Reflecting on certain features of a situation can trigger our deontological instincts; reflecting on other features can trigger our consequentialist instincts. Sometimes—perhaps even usually—these instincts support each other. Sometimes, however, they conflict. These, I think, are simply facts about our moral life. The thought that there must be some unifying source for our moral instincts—one that shows their underlying coherence—strikes me as wholly unlikely on its face.[19] To think otherwise almost certainly arises from the assumption that our moral system, in order to be a system at all, must have an underlying coherent basis. In different words, the tacit assumption of most (though not all) moral theorists is that morality is not dilemma-prone. For my own part, the more I reflect on actual moral problems, the more I am convinced that moral dilemmas are facts of moral life. If this is correct, our systems of moral beliefs are serviceable just to the extent that they are Ludwigean. This claim has two sides: First, a moral system, though dilemma-prone, can provide a reasonable guide for conduct in those areas where dilemmas do not arise. These "safe" areas—as we might call them—may be quite extensive. Second, one of our responsibilities as moral agents is to avoid bringing about moral dilemmas through behaving in morally foolish ways. Foolishly making incompatible promises is one example of this. I should not promise Peter something and Paul something knowing that it is not possible to fulfill both promises. If I am faced with a moral dilemma for this reason, then the fault lies not with the moral system but with me.[20] Unfortunately, the moral systems we live by are not fully Ludwigean. Even when we act with care and goodwill, moral dilemmas can force themselves on us. The decision whether or not to torture the innocent child of a terrorist may provide such an example, at least for some people. It does for me.

I should add that the structure of our moral consciousness is more complicated than this simple contrast between consequentialist and deontological instincts suggests. Conflicts can break out *within* each perspective. Here I will consider only how this can occur within the deontological (rights and duties) standpoint.[21] Our rights and duties are derived from a variety of sources and are applied in a variety of areas. Generally speaking, they are compatible with one another, even support one another. Yet they can come into conflict. In a well-known example, Sartre describes the conflict of a young man faced with the choice between remaining with his aging and bereft mother and leaving her to join the French Resistance. In this case, filial duties come into conflict with patriotic duties. Which take precedence? Sartre claims that no moral theory is capable of resolving this dilemma. The young man has no choice other than to act on his own and in the process define his moral character.[22] I think Sartre is right about this. But Sartre also seems to think that because morality is prone to dilemmas, all moral decisions, down deep, involve such radical choices. This strikes me as just silly and the source of other silliness in Sartre's writings, for example, his claim that there are no innocent victims in war, or that everyone deserves the war he gets. It is essential to see that an irreconcilable moral conflict can exist without bringing all morality down around it. Even if there is no solution to the young man's specific moral dilemma, much of his moral system remains in place. It excludes, for example, the option of neither staying with his mother nor joining the French Resistance but, instead, becoming a ski instructor in Switzerland. Thinking otherwise is almost certainly the result of placing ultrarationalist demands on moral systems: They are either dilemma-free or wholly arbitrary. A leading aim of this work is to break the spell of thinking of that kind. This will take time, however, and, in all likelihood, will never be more than partially successful. The basis for this gloomy prognosis will become more evident in the succeeding chapters.

Before closing this discussion, it may be worth noting that legal systems are clearly dilemma-prone but also (when under the care of a good angel) can be Ludwigean as well. Part of the reason that legal systems are dilemma-prone is that law institutionalizes large portions of morality and in the process incorporates morality's proneness to dilemmas. This is evident, for example, in the legal institution of punishment. The legal institution of punishment is intended to serve multiple purposes, including deterrence, prevention (through incarceration), rehabilitation, and retribution. Sometimes, however, these various purposes do not sit well together. The purposes of deterrence are best served by making prisons extremely miserable places to inhabit. But harsh prison life may not serve the purposes of rehabilitation—indeed, it may run counter to it. To cite another conflict, perhaps surprisingly, the demands of deterrence can run counter to one of the central features of retributivism. A retributive theory of punishment usually contains the following features: (1) a person is punished because he or she deserves to be punished—colloquially, through punishment, the wrongdoer pays for his or her crime; and (2) the degree of punishment is supposed to be commensurate with the seriousness of the crime. This does not mean that the punishment must be equal to the crime—an eye (or its equivalent) for an eye (or its equivalent). It does mean that the most serious crimes should receive the most serious punishments. So far there seems to be a fairly good, though not necessarily perfect, fit between the demands of deterrence and the demands of retribution. Crimes that produce the most harm are threatened with the most harm. The clash between deterrence and retribution arises because of a third feature of the retributive position: (3) the person who has undergone punishment has thereby paid for his or her crime and is, for this reason, free from further legal constraint with respect to that crime. It is this third, seemingly most humane aspect of retributivism that often comes into conflict with the deterrent purposes of punishment. This occurs particularly when the crime in question has a high level of recidivism—as with armed robbery and child molesting. Given the significantly high chance that such people will commit the same crime again, does it make sense to allow them to reenter society no more legally encumbered than any other citizens? A strict retributivist is likely to say yes— once the crime is paid for, that's that. A deterrence theorist is likely to say no—the protection of potential victims overrides the released convict's right to a free and fresh start. Some people find this choice easy (though not always in the same direction). Many people find themselves drawn to some extent to each of these positions and thus, for good reason, are perplexed and troubled.

The more we examine the actual operations of the law, the more dilemma-prone it appears. This is reflected in the almost universal agreement that legal reasoning is fundamentally analogical, not deductive, in character. In saying that legal reasoning is fundamentally analogical in character I do not simply mean that the task of legal reasoning is to show that the facts in the case at hand are more similar to precedents that favor one side of the case than to those that favor the other. There is, of course, a lot of that in our common-law tradition. But analogical reasoning can function in a more dramatic way: It can produce Gestalt changes, globally different and incompatible ways of *appreciating* the same set of facts. Wittgenstein illustrated a phenomenon of this kind using the now famous duck-rabbit diagram:

For most people the diagram alternately looks like a duck, then a rabbit, but never both at once.[23] We can think of a legal debate as one side trying to fix the diagram as a duck and the other side trying to fix it as a rabbit—each side trying to create the illusion that the diagram really *is* determinate in one of these two ways. In this fashion, two people can apprehend the same legal situation in radically different ways; indeed, a particular person—provided she is not engaged as a party to the dispute—can find her views flip-flopping as various aspects of the situation are given prominence.[24] Dwelling on this phenomenon can produce the unsettling feeling that legal decisions are *wholly* baseless.[25] Similar remarks hold for moral reasoning.

But now the question arises: If things are anything like as precarious as I have indicated, how is it that we get along as well as we do? Here I can only hint at the answer that will be developed in later chapters. I think we are saved—to the extent that we are saved—in the same way that the imaginary players of Ludwig were saved. They played a game that was dilemma-prone. Yet the players of Ludwig were not playing *with* the rules, they were playing *within* them. The point of playing the game was to win, and this involved forming strategies, anticipating counterstrategies, and so on. These players, then, were under two sorts of constraints:

1.   The constraints of the rules of Ludwig (a legal move rather than an illegal one)
2.   The constraints imposed by trying to win (a smart move rather than a dumb one)

The fundamental idea is that constraints of the second kind can protect us from (keep us clear of) the paradoxes inherent in the set of rules. Again, we are saved from paradox, to the extent that we are, because we are engaged in rich and stable practical endeavors that keep us clear of regions of paradox.

These reflections, if correct, lead to the result that philosophers (and others) may simply be wrong in trying to find coherent systems of rules underlying our linguistic, moral, and legal institutions. For myself, I no longer think that the assumption of underlying coherence is even a good working hypothesis. Emerson may have been on to something when he said, "A foolish consistency is the hobgoblin of little minds." Here the word "foolish" is crucial. Perhaps Whitman was also on to something with his outburst, "So I contradict myself." This is mere bravado, foolish talk even in a poem, but the reason he gives for contradicting himself—"I am large, I contain multitudes"—is not foolish. Contradiction sometimes arises from inattention or stupidity. We sometimes just fall into contradiction. But contradiction and other forms of incoherence can also arise because we, as human beings, lead complex, multisided lives carrying commitments that cannot be resolved into a coherent unity without severe loss. In "The Crack-Up," F. Scott Fitzgerald wrote, "The test of a first-rate intelligence is the ability to hold two opposed ideas in the mind at the same time and still retain the ability to function." Contradictions of this kind are characteristic of many (perhaps all) great philosophical positions, including those of Plato, Descartes, Spinoza, Hume, Kant, and Wittgenstein (both early and late). All these philosophers were committed to conflicting views that they could not abandon but could not fully reconcile either. Understanding a philosophical position is often a matter of identifying and appreciating the conflicting forces lying within it. When Whitman said in his defense "I am large, I contain multitudes," he may or may not have been accurately describing himself, but he was, in any case, describing many of those philosophers who are still worth taking seriously.

A closing note. Above I have expressed my opinion— an opinion derived largely from Wittgenstein—that the rules that govern human thinking and doing are dilemma-prone and function successfully, to the extent that they do, only because they are Ludwigean. I make no claim to having established these theses; indeed, I have hardly taken any steps in that direction. For example, I have expressed my opinion that no proposed solution to the liar paradox is both technically correct and intuitively plausible. Establishing this would involve a painstaking examination of the wide variety of proposed solutions to show, one by one, that each is inadequate. Even if this were done, it would still leave open the possibility that an adequate solution to the liar paradox may yet be found. I have no idea how this possibility could, in principle, be eliminated. Thus, I have not attempted to *prove* anything in this area (or in the areas of ethics and law) but have instead suggested a way of looking at certain philosophical issues that runs deeply counter to the traditional way of treating them.

These reflections point to a further, more disturbing idea. Not only is philosophy as traditionally pursued incapable of discovering or providing the foundations it seeks, but the philosophical enterprise may itself dislodge the contingent, de facto supports that our daily life depends upon. If that is so, then philosophizing in a certain unrestricted way not only reveals the precariousness of our intellectual life, but actually makes it more precarious. This is the theme of the next two chapters.

Human reason has this peculiar fate that in one species of its knowledge it is burdened by questions which, as prescribed by the very nature of reason itself, it is not able to ignore, but which, as transcending all its powers, it is also not able to answer.

The perplexity into which it thus falls is not due to any fault of its own. It begins with principles which it has no option save to employ in the course of experience, and which this experience at the same time abundantly justifies it in using. Rising with their aid (since it is determined to this also by its own nature) to ever higher, ever more remote, conditions, it soon becomes aware that in this way—the questions never ceasing—its work must always remain incomplete; and it therefore finds itself compelled to resort to principles which overstep all possible empirical employment, and which yet seem so unobjectionable that even ordinary consciousness readily accepts them. But by this procedure human reason precipitates itself into darkness and contradictions.

Immanuel Kant, "Preface A," *Critique of Pure Reason*

CHAPTER THREE

Pure Reason
and Its Illusions

In the previous two chapters I appeared as an ambivalent supporter of reason. I supported reason in the first chapter by claiming that, despite a long history of philosophic claims to the contrary, it is a foolish error to deny the law of noncontradiction. Then, in the second chapter, I seemed to change sides by maintaining that consistency is not an overriding demand—that is, a demand that trumps all others. Specifically, I rejected the principle that we should never employ a system of rules containing an inconsistency until the inconsistency is satisfactorily removed. I also suggested that the threat of inconsistency is a pervasive feature of the rules that govern our cognitive lives. The pervasiveness of such inconsistency is one of the things that make our lives as rational animals precarious.

Clearly I am not a wholehearted rationalist, someone with complete faith in the power of the intellect to expand our understanding of the world around us and to exert a benign control over the lives we lead. This optimistic conception of power of the human mind is associated—in many ways falsely—with the eighteenth-century Enlightenment. As the story is sometimes told, the Enlightenment ideal went out of fashion in the nineteenth century and was refuted in blood in the twentieth. My own view might be called circumspect rationalism. It is the view that our intellectual faculties provide our only means for comprehending the world in which we find ourselves. There is no other reliable access to it. On the other side, the standing threat of contradiction examined in the previous chapter shows that the ideal of a coherent understanding of the world we inhabit is not easily attained and perhaps never fully attainable.

This chapter examines another, more disturbing hindrance to our understanding of ourselves and of our world. Reason, taken on its own terms, not only falls short of satisfying its ideals but actually generates hindrances to its own progress. Though the ancient skeptics anticipated this idea, it was first fully articulated by Hume in one way and then by Kant in another. Both Hume and Kant went beyond the claim that reason is simply too weak to give us complete knowledge of the universe we inhabit—a common theme of ancient skepticism. Both, each in his own way, made the deeper and more disturbing claim that reason, in its purest form, generates illusions that ultimately thwart reason's endeavors. This chapter concentrates on Kant's way of telling this troubling story. The next considers Hume's.

Many of the details of Kant's dauntingly difficult position need not concern us. Here I will concentrate on only two themes central to his philosophy. The first is that the world as we apprehend it is shaped or organized by mind-imposed concepts or categories. The world as it appears to us is not a pure deliverance of the senses but is instead the joint product of what the senses give us and what the mind imposes. The second theme is that the conceptual apparatus that provides this structure to our experience will inevitably lead to intellectual disasters when it is applied to matters completely beyond experience. The passage cited at the head of this chapter forcefully captures this idea that pure reason's "peculiar fate," when unconstrained, is to drive itself "into darkness and contradiction." It is the second theme, Kant's critique of pure reason, that bears most directly on the examination of our precarious life as rational animals, but that theme presupposes the first, so I will begin with it.

For Kant, perception that is not structured by thought is blind, that is, incapable of serving as the basis for knowledge.[1] On this matter, Kant seems to have carried the day. The opposing idea that knowledge is ultimately based on pure experience untainted by thought—a "medium of pure unvarnished news," as Quine calls it— is now almost universally rejected.[2] It is often dismissed out of hand with the label "the myth of the given." This, then, is the first Kantian point: Experience, at least if it is to play a role in knowledge, must be conceptually structured. It is commonly said that this structure or organization is imposed by conceptual frameworks or conceptual schemes.

With respect to conceptual frameworks, we can think of two extreme cases. In what we might call the conservative or closed version, it is held that human experience, at least at its most basic level, is organized under a *single shared framework of categories or basic concepts*. This was Kant's view. He held that the world as apprehended by human beings is a system of unified, mind-introduced structures. These structures include the entire spatiotemporal framework in which we experience events taking place. They also include the system of causal relationships that exist among objects occupying this framework. With respect to these fundamental structures, mind, for Kant, is a lawgiver to nature.[3] Kant further held, and attempted to prove, that these structures are necessary conditions for experience itself and therefore must be shared by all rational creatures who apprehend the world as we do, through experience. We thus have conceptual relativism without conceptual pluralism. Experience is relativized to a categorial framework, but there is no further relativization, at least in any deep respect, to a plurality of possible conceptual schemes. This conservative view of conceptual frameworks has the advantage of providing a basis for mutual intelligibility. If down deep all human beings share the same basic conceptual apparatus—hence the same conception of the basic structure of the world—then it is not surprising that we are able to understand each other even across wide cultural divides.[4]

At the other extreme we have a view that I will call radical relativism or, to use a term now in vogue, radical perspectivism. Protagoras expressed a version of radical perspectivism when he claimed that each individual person is the measure of all things.[5] Nietzsche recommended an extreme version of perspectivism in holding that a person's view of the world is a function of that person's life-affirming or life-denying personality. (Life-affirmers are Heracleiteans; life-deniers are Parmenideans.)[6] The Whorf hypothesis, roughly, the thesis that a culture's worldview is a function of the structure of its language, is another example of perspectivism.[7] Thus, perspectivism comes in a variety of forms, depending on the kind of perspectives the position envisages.

Perspectivism is also embraced by various people who style themselves postmodernists. In its most radical form, perspectivism involves a commitment to claims of the following sort:

A plurality (perhaps an endless plurality) of perspectives is possible.

Every judgment, including judgments about other perspectives, is made from within a perspective.

No perspective is privileged in the sense of being inherently superior to others.

The system of perspectives contains no Archimedean point, that is, it contains no neutral standpoint from which perspectives can be surveyed.

There are no disinterested judges of perspectives.

There is no God's-eye view of the world.

And so on.

Unlike the Kantian version of relativization of experience to concepts, where mutual intelligibility is explicable, radical perspectivists usually insist that people occupying one perspective will find the views of others who occupy radically different perspectives utterly false, stupid, absurd, vicious, or plain nonsense. On this approach, our conceptual schemes wall us off from others enveloped in competing conceptual schemes, thereby producing communication failures on a cosmic scale. When perspectives are relativized to *individual* persons, then conceptual solipsism seems to be the inevitable result. Each of us exists in a state of cranial loneliness, wholly out of touch with what goes on in the heads of others. Failures of communication become the rule, not the exception.[8]

All conceptual relativists, whether conservative or radical, treat objects as constructs. On the contemporary scene there is a widespread tendency to treat objects— perhaps all objects—as social constructs.[9] That some things are social constructs is clear. Money, for example, is a social construct. Without a mutually accepted system of conventions, there would be no such thing as money. Monetary value, as Hume saw long ago, is not a natural value. It is not, however, always obvious whether something is a social construct or not. Locke, for example, thought that property ownership reflected a natural relationship. For him the primordial notion of the ownership of an object is a function of the labor that one puts into it. Marx held a similar view. Hume, in contrast, held that property reflects a conventional relationship determined by the laws that protect people from having things taken from them. Hume argued that many things commonly thought to be natural were, instead, conventional or (to use his word) artificial, but he never abandoned the distinction between the natural and the artificial. He had the good sense to see that convention, to exist at all, must have a basis in something that is not conventional. Conventions, to work, need something nonconventional to build upon and shape. Many writers on the contemporary scene are not blessed with similar good sense. Not only are various human institutions treated as constructs, but biological distinctions and historical events are treated as constructs as well. Not only is being a spouse treated as a social construct, which it is, but so too is gender. Perhaps from an urge to shock, people treat historical events—for example, the Civil War and the Holocaust—as constructs. Sometimes people who speak in this way go on to insist that designating something a construct does not deny its reality, because all things are constructs. But it hardly restores one's sense of reality to be told that the events of the Holocaust are every bit as real as the events related in classical mythology or in children's storybooks.

Perspectivism does not have to be so extreme, though it often is. It is also possible that people who say such batty things are actually misstating or overstating something that might be true and perhaps even important—just as those who deny the law of noncontradiction may, at times, be trying to say something that is correct but are doing so in an utterly inappropriate way. The present task, however, is to assess radical perspectivism taken on its own terms. What should we say about radical perspectivism, working on the assumption that those who present such a view really mean what they say?

There are well-known ways of attacking radical perspectivism and other forms of radical relativism. They often involve ad hominem arguments. The following exchange concerning Protagorean perspectivism occurs in Plato's *Theaetetus*. Socrates describes Protagoras's position in these words:

> He says, does he not, that things are for every man what they seem to him to be?

After it is agreed that Protagoras holds this view, Socrates goes on to apply the Protagorean theory to Protagoras's own doctrine, pointing out, among other things, that it has the following "exquisite" feature:

> *Socrates:* Protagoras admits, I presume, that the contrary opinion about his own opinion (namely, that it is false) must be true, seeing that he agrees that all men judge what is.
>
> *Theodorus:* Undoubtedly.
>
> *Socrates:* And in conceding the truth of the opinion of those who think him wrong, he is really admitting the falsity of his own opinion?
>
> *Theodorus:* Yes, inevitably.
>
> *Socrates:* But for their part the others do not admit that they are wrong?
>
> *Theodorus:* No.[10]

So poor Protagoras must admit that other people are right when they deny what he says, whereas his opponents are under no obligation to make a like concession to Protagoras. I don't think Socrates' argument refutes the Protagorean version of perspectivism—nor do I think that Plato thought it did. There is absolutely no reason why Protagoras cannot dig in his heels and hold that his theory, though true for him, may well be false for others. Far from refuting his theory, this would simply illustrate it.

It simply seems to be a fact that, under certain circumstances, radical perspectivism can seem compellingly true. Despite the lack of any good arguments in its behalf, one can be drawn irresistibly to it. We feel the urge to say, "Everything is relative"—investing these words with a particular ring of profundity. In this mood it doesn't even seem necessary to specify just what everything is supposed to be relative *to*. We feel a general sense of the relativity of things; how the details are worked out is correspondingly less important.[11] Here is an actual example of someone sliding, for no apparent reason, into a linguistic version of radical perspectivism. As a graduate student, I heard a distinguished French physicist lecturing on the philosophy of science. In the midst of saying interesting things about the philosophical problems raised by quantum mechanics, he felt called on to make the following aside:

> But of course, the sky was not blue before someone called it "blue."

When a French intellectual says "but of course" in that particularly French shrug-of-the-shoulders sort of way, it is a sure sign that something perfectly outrageous is about to follow, as in this case it did. Looking about me, I saw a number of heads nodding in agreement and not a single person showing stunned disbelief that a distinguished physicist could utter such a transparent physical falsehood. Pressing him on the matter, I asked if he really thought that at some time in the past a person called the sky blue and then (*voilà!*), because of his doing so, the sky took on that hue. If so, what conceivable physical account could be given of such an extraordinary event? How could uttering the words "That's blue" (or "C'est bleu") bring about a fundamental change in the diffraction properties of the upper atmosphere? He replied that he intended his remark to be taken philosophically, not scientifically. Under further pressure he retreated to what amounted to the claim that the sky was not called blue until it was called blue—which is true enough. He was discomfited; I was pleased.

Forty years later I am still a bit pleased—I wouldn't tell the story if I weren't. Yet it is now clear to me that I did not address the really important questions:

> Why is there a temptation to think that something is profoundly true when, taken straightforwardly, it is obviously false?
>
> How does it happen that the obvious falsehood seems not to matter—seems trivial in comparison with the profundity of the point being made?

Why do commonsense or even scientific refutations
seem wholly ineffective against such claims?

When Samuel Johnson kicks a stone in an attempt to refute
Berkeley's view that no material objects exist, the idealist
replies that Johnson, far from refuting Berkeley, has not
even proven the existence of his own foot. A person who
claims to have shown that time is unreal remains unmoved
by the rhetorical question "Just when did you prove this?"
The same situation holds for various forms of radical
perspectivism. Pointing out that these positions run
counter to common sense cuts no ice because the whole
point of adopting such views is to undermine or unmask
common sense.

In fact, I do not think there is any direct way of refuting
radical perspectivism—just as there is no way of directly
refuting those who refuse to accept the law of noncontradiction. Both maneuvers seal themselves off from refutation, though in different ways. Denying the law of
noncontradiction in effect undercuts all argumentation,
including refutation. Radical perspectivism achieves the
same result by making any claim or argument as good as
any other. In doing so, it makes the rebuttal "Yeah, that's
what you say" a complete stopper.[12] Instead of trying to
refute radical perspectivism, I think we have to go deeper
and attempt to find its sources.

Kant provides such diagnosis. I find this the deepest
aspect of his philosophy. We have already noted that Kant
was the first philosopher to give a fully systematic statement
of the doctrine that our view of the world is shaped or

conditioned by the conceptual scheme we impose on it. Though Kant was not himself a radical perspectivist, it was from this seed that radical perspectivism grew. We reach radical perspectivism by replacing Kant's single, necessary categorial scheme with a plurality of competing categorial schemes. Kant, however, appended a warning about the misuse of categories that organize our experience: It is only in conjunction with something that is *not* conceptual that these categories find legitimate employment. It is precisely this constraint that many of our contemporary perspectivists ignore. They fail to see that the relationship between concepts and percepts is reciprocal. Again, as Kant put it, "percepts without concepts are blind," but, as he further adds, "concepts without percepts are empty." Here Kant rather understates his own position. For him, concepts without percepts are not simply empty, but sometimes dangerous. This is the second fundamental thesis of Kant's position given at the start of this chapter: Our conceptual apparatus, when unconstrained by experience, generates intellectual disasters.

As Kant saw, there are strong drives that push us toward employing our concepts in ways that are not constrained by experience—that is, giving them, as he says, pure or empirically unfettered employment. One problem with relying on experience is that it is largely out of our control, and views based on it are always open to future refutation. Later, John Dewey made a similar point when he identified our quest for certainty—our quest for total assurance—as the source of our metaphysical longings.[13] More deeply— and this is the point that Kant primarily stresses—empirical knowledge always strikes us as incomplete, always leaving questions unanswered. Empirical knowledge concerns the world as it happens to be. Told that the universe is governed by certain physical laws, someone committed to rational ideals wants to know why these laws obtain rather than others. We naturally want to know whether these laws are ultimate or, perhaps, based on other even deeper laws. When such deeper laws are discovered, the same questions are simply renewed. The inherent incompleteness of all empirical explanations can, in the end, make the world seem, at its root, fundamentally unintelligible. In contrast to Pope's celebratory couplet in his *Essay on Man:*

> Nature, and Nature's laws lay hid in night.
> God said Let Newton be! and all was light,

Hume saw more deeply when he remarked:

> While Newton seemed to draw off the veil from some
> of the mysteries of nature, he shewed at the same time
> the imperfections of the mechanical philosophy; and
> thereby restored her ultimate secrets to that obscurity,
> in which they ever did and ever will remain.[14]

Basic empirical laws, even if discovered, will strike human reason as merely brute, hence unsatisfactory even if true.

Because of our desire for certainty and, more deeply, because of our desire for complete, unconditioned knowledge, the mind, according to Kant, naturally attempts to liberate its concepts from their empirical limitations. We thus enter, in his words, into the project of pure reason. The result, according to Kant, is inevitable intellectual disaster. Freed from empirical constraints, our discussions are reduced, as he says, to

> mere talk—in which, with a certain plausibility, we maintain, or, if such be our choice, attack, any and every possible assertion.[15]

In Kant's words, reason has now turned dialectical. We have nothing but mere talk confronting mere talk.

The passage just cited has another important feature: Kant speaks of a certain plausibility attaching to the results of such pure reflection. These dialectical illusions, as Kant noticed, share an important feature with perceptual illusions: Though we can take measures not to be fooled by them, their illusory appeal cannot be reasoned away. The Müller-Lyer diagram illustrates this. If we ignore the tails, line A clearly looks longer than line B.

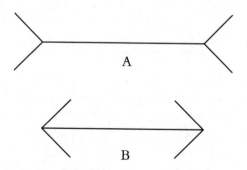

If we measure these lines, we discover that A and B are equal in length. But even though we now *know* that their lengths are the same, this does not change the way they *look* to us. It is not in our intellectual power to change their look. According to Kant, we are in the same situation with respect to intellectual illusions—illusions imposed on us not by perception, but by pure reason. Even after we have learned to recognize these illusions and guard against them, they still present themselves as speciously alluring. In fact, intellectual illusions present problems more recalcitrant than those posed by perceptual illusions. Most people have no conception of intellectual illusions and therefore are not alert to the deep mischief they can produce. This includes many philosophers who, since Kant has sounded the warning, ought to know better. Furthermore, perceptual illusions usually present themselves as mere curiosities, whereas intellectual illusions carry with them a sense of importance and depth. Perceptual illusions can usually be detected using straightforward, commonsense procedures, whereas intellectual illusions are case-hardened against good sense. Most troublesome of all, intellectual illusions can lie completely unnoticed in the background, distorting and unhinging our thoughts without our having any sense that this is happening.

Because Kant thought it was possible to give a complete account of the mind's underlying conceptual structure, he also thought it possible to give a complete account of the kinds of intellectual illusions that arise from the misuse of our conceptual apparatus.[16] His leading idea was this: When we employ fundamental categories without empirical constraints, we can be captured by the idea that we have encountered necessary structures of the world itself rather than simply the structures necessary to give a coherent representation of the world.[17]

Kant held that three imposing, but thoroughly bogus, edifices have their foundations in the pure use—hence misuse—of basic categories of experience. These are the fields of *rational cosmology,* which concerns the nature and origin of the physical world; *rational psychology,* which concerns the nature, in particular the immortality, of the human soul; and *rational theology,* which concerns the nature and existence of God. Each of these fields presents us with proofs that, though invalid, can still strike us, at least under certain circumstances, as deeply persuasive. Indeed, these proofs are often so transparently invalid that it is hard to understand how anyone could seriously put them forward for acceptance. Yet it remains true that many people able to tell the difference between an invalid proof and a valid one can persist in thinking that, despite the surface invalidity, certain proofs, say, for the existence of God, contain important insights underlying them. The feeling can persist, even if we cannot articulate it, that somehow we are in possession of a proof of God's existence. Kant, for his part, would have none of this. For him, theoretical proofs of the existence of God are impossible, and the thought that down deep there must be something to them exhibits nothing more than the persistent influence of an intellectual illusion.[18]

One of Kant's most important ideas is that intellectual illusions often occur as competing, incompatible pairs. One kind of illusion inclines us to accept as necessary the existence of absolute or unconditioned beings, whereas illusions on the other side incline us to the polar opposite view that everything is wholly relative and conditioned. We think that there must be an *ultimate* ground for the existence of things—else, we are tempted to think, nothing could exist at all. But as soon as we identify something as an ultimate ground, that is, as soon as we make it an object of thought and scrutinize it, we seem driven to inquire into *its* ground. Because of this competition between opposing illusions, Kant speaks of *dialectical* illusions. They are of special importance to us because they often lie behind, and seemingly make urgent, the radical choices mentioned in the introduction. As long as the radical choice is accepted, the rejection of one of the illusions commits us to the other. What has to be seen is that the choice between illusions is itself an illusory choice.

This tendency to yo-yo from one side to another of a dialectical choice is illustrated in an exchange in Hume's *Dialogues Concerning Natural Religion*. Cleanthes, a representative of natural religion, has presented a rather standard version of the argument from design—the so-called teleological proof of God's existence. Roughly, the order, beauty, and organization of the world are intelligible only on the assumption that it was created by an intelligent being. On these grounds Cleanthes rests his proof of a deity. In response, Philo, the "careless"—that is, carefree—skeptic, simply pushes the inquiry one step further back by asking:

> How . . . shall we satisfy ourselves concerning the cause of that Being whom you suppose the Author of Nature,

or, according to your system of Anthropomorphism, the ideal world, into which you trace the material? Have we not the same reason to trace that ideal world into another ideal world, or new intelligent principle?[19]

To which Cleanthes answers:

The order and arrangement of nature, the curious adjustment of final causes, the plain use and intention of every part and organ; all these bespeak in the clearest language an intelligent cause or author. The heavens and the earth join in the same testimony: the whole chorus of Nature raises one hymn to the praises of its Creator. You alone, or almost alone, disturb this general harmony. You start abstruse doubts, cavils, and objections: you ask me, what is the cause of this cause? I know not; I care not; that concerns not me. I have found a Deity; and here I stop my enquiry. Let those go further, who are wiser or more enterprising.[20]

And Philo replies:

I pretend to be neither, . . . and for that very reason, I should never perhaps have attempted to go so far; especially when I am sensible, that I must at last be contented to sit down with the same answer, which, without further trouble, might have satisfied me from the beginning. If I am still to remain in utter ignorance of causes, and can absolutely give an explication of nothing, I shall never esteem it any advantage to shove

off for a moment a difficulty, which, you acknowledge,
must immediately, in its full force, recur upon me.[21]

We should not allow the ease and elegance of Hume's
writing to mask the depth of his insights. When he has
Cleanthes declare "I have found a Deity; and here I stop
my enquiry," Hume captures the demand for closure
overriding what is, after all, a perfectly good criticism. The
important feature of Philo's response is its complete generality: It applies to any causal argument whatsoever, not
simply to Cleanthes' causal argument for God's existence.
Because the quest for causes of causes has no termination,
each causal explanation can never do more than "shove off
for a moment a difficulty, which . . . must immediately, in
its full force, recur upon [us]."

Kant calls such competitions between opposing illusions
antinomies. The first antinomy he examines turns on the
question whether the world did or did not have a beginning
in time. The thesis of the first antinomy is that it had to have
a beginning in time; the antithesis is that it could not have.
Starting with the thesis, why would someone think that the
world could not have existed forever in time? The answer,
put rather crudely, is that if the world existed forever in time,
then there would be no ultimate reason why it should have
existed at all. Admittedly, we might be able to explain why
the world existed at one time by connecting this causally to
its existence at some prior time. This, however, takes us
nowhere because it leaves wholly inexplicable why the causal
chain exists at all. Here the voice of reason is speaking with
its demand for the unconditioned, for the finished-off.

Turning now to the antithesis, let us consider the possibility that the world did have a beginning in time. We are unavoidably led to ask what caused it to begin at *that* time rather than at any other. On the view maintained in the thesis, we are asked to consider an endless, homogeneous stretch of empty time suddenly interrupted by the appearance of the world. Because any time is as good as any other for the appearance of the world, there seems to be no way in principle of answering the question: Why then rather than some time else? It hardly seems to help to bring God into the picture, for a homogeneous stretch of eventless time provides no grounds, even for God, for creating a world at one time rather than at another. (Saying that the ways of God are not the ways of man simply throws in the towel.) Here the voice of critical understanding is speaking, rejecting all attempts at closure.

This dialectical impasse has a number of interesting features. First, the thesis and the antithesis each proceed by attempting to reduce its opposite to absurdity. In the thesis, reflecting on a world existing endlessly back into the past is supposed to reveal the absurdity of such an idea. In the antithesis, reflecting on a world popping into existence at one time rather than another is supposed to strike us as utterly arbitrary. A second important feature of the thesis and the antithesis is that each relies on something like a principle of sufficient reason—only they apply it at different levels. In the thesis the principle is applied globally: There must be a single ultimate ground for the whole works, for the entire causal chain. In the antithesis, it is applied to things taken individually—each and every thing must have its ground in something else. For those who are attracted by the antithesis, contingency goes all the way back. Like Philo in Hume's *Dialogues,* we never stop asking for causes.

Well, who is right? Did the world have a beginning in time or not? I do not know the answer to this question and I do not think anyone else knows the answer either, but I hope one thing is clear: This issue cannot be settled by dialectical reasoning of the kind just examined. This issue will not be solved by favoring one dialectical illusion over its competitor. It will be solved, if it is solved at all, through considering such things as the total mass of the universe, its rate of expansion, and so on. If the issue is going to be resolved, it will have to be resolved scientifically. Such a solution will not satisfy our metaphysical yearnings. If, for example, some version of the Big Bang theory is eventually accepted on scientific grounds, it will strike many as being thoroughly counterintuitive. For such people, if the Big Bang occurred, then (science be damned) something, perhaps God, must have caused it. It is odd but true that some people find religious solace in the Big Bang theory.

For the most part, Kant stresses that reason, when it turns dialectical, posits immutable basic entities. These are the standard inhabitants of traditional a priori metaphysics: God, souls, Platonic ideas, Democritean indestructible atoms, and the like. It is, however, important to remember, as our brief examination of Kant's first antinomy shows, that reason, in its dialectical mode, can proceed in the opposite direction, rejecting all determinacy, all completeness, all closure. Dialectical illusions of this kind provide, I suggest, the deeper account for the attractiveness, the compelling nature, of radical perspectivism. Dialectical reasoning does not simply produce a seemingly irresistible dogma, for example, that a necessary being must exist; rather, to return to an earlier theme, it presents us with a radical choice: Either an absolutely necessary being exists or everything is absolutely contingent (accidental, a jumble, a mere heap, a mess). Or again: Either an absolute standpoint exists (the God's-eye view) or endlessly many perspectives exist, each as acceptable or unacceptable as any other.

What we discover, remarkably enough, is that people accept radical perspectivism in the same a priori, absolutist spirit that old-fashioned metaphysicians formerly accepted the existence of God. Their views are the same in being products of dialectical illusions. We have absolute absolutism squared off against absolute relativism. Whether the illusion resides in the positive or the negative pole is of little interest to us; the common source of these extreme commitments is. If we step back and avoid partisanship, we see that these primal opponents, properly understood, are fundamentally more similar than different.

As already mentioned, dialectical illusions often operate in the background, exerting their influence without being recognized by those under their spells. There are, however, various clear signs showing that dialectical illusions are at work. With respect to the positive illusions—those that lead one to posit necessary beings of one sort or another—there is a willingness to accept perfectly awful proofs in behalf of the existence of their prized entities. There is always the problem—often brushed aside—of explaining how the posited ideal entities are related to our nonideal world. For example, if a god created the world simply by uttering the words "Let there be . . . ," then we are confronted with a mode of manufacture wholly unintelligible to us, so the proposed explanation is no explanation at all. If, on the other hand, a god created the world in a manner similar to the way a watchmaker makes a watch, then we know what to look for: marks of manufacture, say, things bolted together or a stray tool accidentally left behind.[22] No one, so far as I know, has ever taken this route to prove the existence of God; indeed, those who defend the argument from design would consider it mere parody to pitch it at this level. "We are not," they will say, "seeking a god in the image of Thomas Alva Edison." Of course they are not. For the argument from design to be persuasive, it is essential to keep the conception of God and his, her, or its relationship to the world as indeterminate as possible. Emptiness and lack of specificity are standard marks of dialectical illusions on the positive side of a dialectical choice.

There are also some clear signs that thought has turned dialectical in a negative way. One is a tendency to present a plain falsehood as a deep truth ("The sky was not blue until someone called it blue"). Another is a tendency (conscious or not) to make claims that are either self-refuting or self-stultifying. Consider the claim that there is no such thing as meaning. If true, it is meaningless, but that which is meaningless cannot be true. For that matter, if meaningless, it cannot be false either. The next step in this bizarre development is to reject the notions of truth and falsehood, and the law of noncontradiction with them. With Kant as our tutor, it should be clear what is happening here: We have before us a new kind of absolutism, one that inverts the positive absolutism of traditional metaphysics, yielding an absolute relativism. Radical relativism in its various forms—whether Protagorean or postmodernist—bears all the marks of reason turning dialectical. It deals in the absolutist coin that it mistakenly claims to reject.

&

In the *Critique of Pure Reason,* Kant employs the wonderful image of a dove complaining that air resistance slows it down.

> The light dove, cleaving the air in her free flight, and feeling its resistance, might imagine that its flight would be still easier in empty space. It was thus that Plato left the world of the senses, as setting too narrow limits to the understanding, and ventured out beyond it on the wings of the ideas, in the empty space of the pure understanding. He did not observe that with all his efforts he made no advance—meeting no resistance that might, as it were, serve as a support upon which he could take a stand, to which he could apply his powers, and so set his understanding in motion.[23]

Continuing this metaphor, we should always ask how a particular position gets air under its wings. How can it fly? The answer cannot be that the air is always supplied by other wings. Dropping the metaphor, we want to know how concepts can be controlled in their application by something that is not merely conceptual. This, it seems, is the only way to prevent thought from turning dialectical, in either its positive or its negative form. If we are going to engage in methodology, its fundamental question must be this: What constraints prevent a particular discipline from becoming merely dialectical? If the answer to this question is nothing, this by itself shows that the discipline has lost systematic connection with its subject matter and, as a discipline, is no more than an illusion. Those who practice such a discipline should blush.

If this broadly Kantian story that I have told is correct, then we have found yet another source of the precariousness of our life as rational animals. In the second chapter I argued that the systems of rules that govern our intellectual activities are pervasively dilemma-prone, that is, they contain inconsistencies (and other forms of incoherence) that are not easily eliminated and perhaps never wholly eliminable. In this chapter I have noted, following Kant, that our conceptual apparatus has an inherent tendency to rise above empirical restraints, with the result that our heads are filled with deeply entrenched intellectual fantasies—fantasies made more dangerous through masquerading as profound and irresistible truths.

To deal with both these problems—the inherent inconsistency of the systems of rules that govern our thought, and the tendency for thought to turn dialectical—we must, I have suggested, find some way of constraining the conceptual by the nonconceptual. I don't think Kant was able to answer this, his own question. I'm not sure I can either. But before making that effort at amelioration, another threat to our lives as rational animals has to be considered: the challenge of skepticism.

Sceptical doubt, both with respect to reason and the senses, is a malady, which can never be radically cur'd, but must return upon us every moment, however we may chace it away, and sometimes may seem entirely free from it. 'Tis impossible upon any system to defend either our understanding or senses; and we but expose them farther when we endeavour to justify them in that manner. As the sceptical doubt arises naturally from a profound and intense reflection on those subjects, it always encreases, the farther we carry our reflections, whether in opposition or conformity to it.

David Hume, *Treatise of Human Nature*

CHAPTER FOUR

Skepticism

This work concerns the precarious life of a particular animal species, *Homo sapiens*. We have noted two ways in which our rational life is precarious. First, under close scrutiny, we discover that many of the belief systems we rely on are inconsistent in the sense that in certain circumstances they yield contradictory or conflicting results. Many of these inconsistencies prove stubborn, that is, hard to remove in a satisfactory way—hard to remove without our being forced to give things up that we would like to keep. These inconsistencies are also pervasive. They crop up almost across the board, even in places where we would least expect them—in such supposedly safe zones as logic and mathematics. We seem to live our intellectual lives on the edge of absurdity.

In the previous chapter we examined a second source of intellectual peril: When confronted with its limitations, the human mind has a tendency to turn dialectical—using this expression in Kant's, not Plato's or Hegel's, sense of that word. As a result, we are captured by dialectical illusions that distort our thinking in fundamental ways. Kant, for his part, was primarily concerned with exposing the illusions driving the a priori metaphysics of his predecessors. Such metaphysical theories presented the world—at least in its really real aspects—as a necessary, unalterable structure. I have called dialectical illusions of this kind illusions of absolutism. Though they are still around—they are always around—I have said relatively little about illusions of this kind. Instead, I have concentrated on dialectical illusions of the reverse kind, those that lead one to see the world as having no nonarbitrary structure at all, for it is this kind of illusion that pervades our contemporary intellectual culture. I have labeled dialectical illusions of this second kind illusions of relativism, or illusions of perspectivism. Though opposites, both illusions of absolutism and illusions of relativism are barriers to inquiry. In this chapter I will examine a third threat to our lives as rational animals: the tendency of reason, when left to its own devices, to be driven into radical forms of skepticism. With the addition of skepticism, we complete the trinity of threats to our rational lives: inconsistency, illusion, and doubt.

The word "skeptic" can trigger a variety of associations, many of them inappropriate. A standard misunderstanding is that the skeptic is a denier or naysayer. Skeptics often *suspend* judgment on matters commonly believed, but this is different from denying these beliefs. A skeptic about the existence of God does not deny that God exists—that is atheism, not skepticism. Another mistake is to confuse skepticism with cynicism. Cynics are usually unswerving in their commitment to a moral ideal, but disappointed or disgusted by humanity's failure to meet it. The cynic Diogenes would recognize an honest man if he met one but despairs of ever doing so. Skeptics have no such dogmatic commitment to a moral ideal and, generally speaking, are not harsh in their judgments of their fellow human beings. Finally, skepticism may suggest a gloomy, negative attitude toward life. There have been gloomy skeptics, but skepticism has also been recommended for the peace of mind, even cheerfulness, it brings. Someone, I do not know who, has drawn a distinction between East Coast skeptics and West Coast skeptics. East Coast skeptics recognize that their knowledge is limited, and this troubles them deeply. West Coast skeptics recognize the same thing but find it liberating. Using this classification, the ancient skeptics are mostly West Coast skeptics, modern skeptics are mostly East Coast skeptics. I am on the side of the ancients.

With these common misunderstandings out of the way, we can next note that skepticism is a complex position that comes in various forms. One distinction will be crucial for understanding what follows. I have spoken of a skeptic as one who suspends judgment concerning certain beliefs. There is, however, another way of characterizing skepticism that is often connected with suspension of belief but is still different from it. A skeptic is someone who calls into question the basis or justification of some system of belief.

In this sense, a religious skeptic challenges the justification for religious beliefs, and a moral skeptic challenges the basis for moral beliefs. These challenges typically take the form of skeptical arguments, arguments that, if not refuted, show that we are not justified in believing certain things that people commonly do believe. It will be useful to have a name for these two sorts of skepticism. For skepticism that involves suspension of belief, we can speak of *belief skepticism*. Because the other kind of skepticism challenges justification, we will call it, for want of a better name, *justification skepticism*.

Belief skepticism and justification skepticism are related in an obvious way: Generally speaking, we ought not to believe things that we are not justified in believing. The nineteenth-century figure G. K. Clifford gave a heroic statement of this principle by declaring, "It is wrong always, everywhere, and for anyone, to believe anything upon insufficient evidence."[1] If this principle is correct, then one ought to abandon beliefs when they are recognized to be unjustified. We can call this Clifford's principle.

At first sight, Clifford's principle may seem obviously true, yet in a variety of ways it has been rejected. Fideism, the view that faith, even when contrary to reason, can provide an adequate basis for belief, is one example. The fideist holds that reason is not capable of establishing such things as the existence of God and the immortality of the soul, holding instead that religious beliefs can be founded only on faith. Indeed, a true fideist would find it appalling if the existence of God could be established on the basis of reason alone. The fideist, then, is a justification skeptic concerning the possibility of providing rational grounds for belief in God's existence but is not a belief skeptic on the matter.[2] Somewhat differently, the paranoid may recognize intellectually that some of his beliefs are unfounded but still not be able to shake them. However, irrational cases such as paranoia are not the concern of this study; it is concerned with the perils of rationality, not irrationality. We are concerned not with irrational departures from Clifford's principle, but instead with the consequences that arise from embracing it wholeheartedly and without reservation. The result—though this is the last thing Clifford intended—is a radical justification skepticism that may bring belief skepticism in its train. The claim, then, is that Clifford's principle, fully embraced, generates skepticism with regard to justification. To see how this happens, we will examine in turn three forms of skepticism: cartesian skepticism, Humean skepticism, and Pyrrhonian skepticism.

Cartesian skepticism. The first thing to note about cartesian skepticism is that the label "cartesian skepticism" is a misnomer. René Descartes was not a skeptic; he was an antiskeptic. The lowercase spelling of "cartesian" is an effort to respect this fact. Descartes's concern with skeptical arguments came about in the following way. In his *Meditations on First Philosophy,* Descartes sets himself the task of trying to find an absolutely secure basis for knowledge. In pursuit of this goal, he adopts the following methodological strategy: He will accept something as true only if it remains secure under the most unfavorable circumstances imaginable. To this end, he tells us:

> I will suppose therefore that . . . some malicious demon
> of the utmost power and cunning has employed all his
> energies in order to deceive me. I shall think that the
> sky, the air, the earth, colours, shapes, sounds and all
> external things are merely the delusions of dreams which
> he has devised to ensnare my judgement. I shall consider
> myself as not having hands or eyes, or flesh, or blood or
> senses, but as falsely believing that I have all these things.
> I shall stubbornly and firmly persist in this meditation;
> and, even if it is not in my power to know any truth, I
> shall at least do what is in my power, that is, resolutely
> guard against assenting to any falsehoods, so that the
> deceiver, however powerful and cunning he may be,
> will be unable to impose on me in the slightest degree.[3]

Contemporary philosophers update this example by asking their readers to consider the possibility that they are
no more than brains suspended in a liquid-filled vat, with
all of their experiences being induced in them by brain
probes. The trick here, of course, is that the world might
look no different from within the vat than it looks to us
now, presumably when we are not in such a vat. It thus
seems perfectly impossible for a person to establish that he
is not a brain in a vat. It may be similarly impossible for a
person to prove that she is not dreaming or not mad or
not deceived by a malicious demon. Skeptical challenges
of this kind are now called *skeptical scenarios*. When I speak
of cartesian skepticism (with a lowercase "c") I have in
mind versions of skepticism that employ such skeptical
scenarios.

Under certain circumstances people can be led to take skeptical scenarios seriously, and when they do, they can find them deeply troubling. To see how we can be led into such perplexity, we can begin by examining an ordinary, nonphilosophical setting where a reasonable doubt can be raised. The following exchange might take place in a trial:

Q: You claim to know that Mr. X was in New York on the evening of March fifteenth?

A: Yes sir.

Q: How do you know this?

A: He came into the restaurant where I was dining, just as I was leaving.

Q: You are well acquainted with him?

A: Yes, he works in the same department I do, just a few desks away.

Q: Did you speak to each other?

A: No.

Q: I wonder if you know that Mr. X has a twin brother?

A: No, I never heard of a twin brother.

Q: One who also lives in New York?

A: I had no idea.

Q: So, for all you know, it may have been Mr. X's twin brother you saw.

A: I suppose that's possible.

Q: So you really do not know that it was Mr. X whom you saw?

A: I suppose not.

This exchange begins with A offering perfectly standard reasons for thinking that he correctly identified Mr. X as being present in the restaurant: He is personally acquainted with Mr. X and could plainly see him. Typically we expect no more than this. Then, having gotten A to acknowledge that no words were exchanged, Q introduces the fact that Mr. X has a twin brother living in the same city. In the philosophical trade this maneuver is called introducing a *defeator* to a knowledge claim. In the given context, a defeator is a relevant consideration that must be eliminated for a knowledge claim to be acceptable. In general, a knowledge claim is legitimate only if *all* relevant defeators have been eliminated. Suppose in our example that A *had* spoken with the person he took to be Mr. X. This would change things in an important way. In even a brief conversation, it would, in all likelihood, soon become clear whether or not this was the person he worked with, rather than his twin look-alike. But no such conversation took place, and A relied simply on the appearance of the person he took to be Mr. X. Once the possibility of a twin is introduced, this evidence is not good enough to support A's claim to know that the person he saw in the restaurant was the person he works with.

These reflections show that our ordinary knowledge claims are governed by what I have elsewhere called levels of scrutiny.[4] I will try to explain this notion more carefully at the close of this chapter, but it will be useful to introduce it informally here. In making knowledge claims, we are supposed to have eliminated all relevant defeators. But what makes certain defeators relevant and others not relevant?

This is not an easy question to answer, but clearly in daily life we *do* recognize the difference between relevant and irrelevant defeators and implicitly rely on this distinction. To go back to the exchange between Q and A, suppose instead of pointing out that Mr. X has a twin brother, Q simply raises this as a possibility by asking, "Isn't it possible that Mr. X has a twin brother who also lives in New York?" In response, A would have every right to ask in return, "Is there any reason to suppose that he does?" Generally speaking, we are not expected to eliminate such a remote possibility when identifying someone. Things change, however, when the fact is introduced that Mr. X *does* have a twin brother who lives in the same city. The level of scrutiny rises, for what would normally count as a remote defeator now becomes a relevant defeator in need of elimination.

We are supposed to eliminate all relevant defeators (not every possible defeator) when making a claim to knowledge. Eliminating every possible defeator would present us with an enormous task that, in most cases, would be impossible to complete. Furthermore, that a potential defeator is easy to check on does not, by itself, provide a reason for considering it. For example, as I sit in my room, it might strike me that someone could have left a large packing crate in front of my door. If so, I am wrong in thinking that I know that I have plenty of time to meet a friend for lunch. There is no difficulty in checking on this; I need only open the door—or try to. So, to be on the safe side, maybe I should. There are, however, endlessly many other worries of the same kind that would overwhelm me if I took them seriously. (Perhaps someone has glued my lock in a closed position; perhaps there is now a gaping hole outside my door.) In making knowledge claims—indeed, in the general conduct of one's life—it is essential, not just a good idea, to ignore defeators unless something specifically triggers a concern for them. To do otherwise would paralyze our activities. This, I think, is what Wittgenstein had in mind when he wrote:

> My *life* consists in my being content to accept many things.[5]

In contrast, anyone who accepted Clifford's principle in a literal and unrestricted way would find his or her life in shambles—in fact, unlivable.

We can now return to skeptical scenarios, with their reliance on deceiving demons, brains in vats, and the like. There are two main differences between evaluating knowledge claims in these circumstances and evaluating them in everyday circumstances. First, skeptical scenarios deal in wildly remote defeating possibilities, with the result that the level of scrutiny becomes unrestrictedly high. Second, skeptical scenarios typically deal with defeators that, it seems, are in principle uneliminable. We can consider these two differences in turn.

As we saw above, in daily life we do not attempt to eliminate many unlikely defeators even when they are easily eliminated. We do not take them seriously—and rightly so. Yet many philosophers have taken the ultraremote defeators found in skeptical scenarios seriously. The question is why. The brief answer is that they are doing philosophy in a traditional way that is uncompromising in its commitment to a rational ideal. Recall Descartes's methodological use of the malicious demon. In his attempt to find knowledge that was absolutely secure, he made the standards of acceptance hyperbolically high. He did not start out by doubting *everything,* as some have carelessly put it. Instead, he decided to set aside any belief against which even the slightest possible doubt could be raised. In different words, he placed no limits on the range of possible defeators. Only those beliefs that prove bulletproof against doubt of this kind would count as perfectly secure knowledge—knowledge that could serve as the secure foundation for an edifice of knowledge.

Descartes's efforts did not prove successful. He did find at least one belief that even a malicious demon could not undercut, namely, his belief in his own existence. The demon could destroy even this belief by destroying Descartes himself, but as long as the demon keeps Descartes around as someone to deceive, at least this one belief, it seems, will be secure. That is progress, but it is important to see how little progress it is. Descartes, for example, has no reason to think that a human being named René Descartes exists, no reason to think that he has a physical body, no reason for thinking that anything else of any kind exists, and so forth. He starts out in a state of cranial loneliness—if he has a cranium. His situation is so dire that it takes nothing short of a deity to extract him from it. (When in trouble, philosophers, like ordinary folks, often raise their eyes to heaven.) Specifically,

Descartes attempted to prove the existence of a god who, being perfect, would neither deceive nor allow a deceiver to inhabit the universe. Many have thought that Descartes's attempted proof of God's existence is circular, and even if not circular, in any case no good. If that is right, then Descartes has scored only a small victory over the malicious demon (and hence skepticism), the justified belief in the existence of his (or her or its) own mind together with some knowledge of the immediate contents of this mind. The deceiving demon wins everything else. There is an irony here. Descartes, as already noted, was not a skeptic; he viewed himself as an enemy of skepticism. Yet, in the end, he bequeathed to the world a fundamental challenge to knowledge that goes by the name of cartesian skepticism.

The first feature of skeptical scenarios is that they deal with wildly remote defeating possibilities. A second feature of skeptical scenarios that also sets them apart from everyday epistemic contexts is that they present, or at least seem to present, defeators that are *in principle* uneliminable. It seems at least possible that I am a brain in a vat with my experiences being given to me via brain probes controlled by extremely clever neuroscientists. These clever neuroscientists stimulate parts of the brain in a way that produces experiences that are indistinguishable from the experiences that a person has when actually perceiving the world. So my present experience of a computer screen seemingly before me may have come to me via the senses or by way of brain probes, and if the neuroscientists are sufficiently clever, I may have no way of distinguishing one from the other. That seems to imply that right now, for all I know, I may be such an envatted brain. The hypothesis that I am seems invulnerable to refutation.

This feature of invulnerability has been viewed as both the strength and the weakness of skeptical scenarios. If to know something one must eliminate all possible defeators and there are some defeators that are, in principle, uneliminable, then knowledge—at least in those areas where the defeators apply—is impossible. Some, however, have argued that this supposed strength of skeptical scenarios is really a fatal weakness. For a doubt to be genuine or meaningful, it is sometimes said, there must be some way, at least in principle, of resolving it. If that is right, then doubts generated by skeptical scenarios are empty doubts or pseudodoubts. Wittgenstein makes the point this way in the *Tractatus:*

> Scepticism is *not* irrefutable, but obviously nonsensical, when it tries to raise doubts where no questions can be asked.
>
> For doubt can exist only where a question exists, a question only where an answer exists, and an answer only where something *can be said.*[6]

Over the years a great many variations have been rung on this theme. I will simply report that I find this maneuver unpersuasive. I think that I perfectly well understand skeptical scenarios, and in understanding them I find them completely unanswerable.[7] My attitude here parallels my attitude toward the liar paradox discussed in chapter 2. Not only do I find this skeptical challenge unanswerable, I think it is perfectly clear why it is unanswerable.

We know why Descartes became involved with skeptical scenarios: He did so for methodological reasons. It was an attempt to find a completely secure base for knowledge by defeating skepticism on its own grounds. Given the failure of Descartes's project, why do other philosophers concern themselves with skeptical scenarios? Why, for example, has there been so much written on this topic over the past thirty years or so? What is driving this interest? I'm not sure I know the answer to this question—I certainly do not know the whole answer. Part of the answer, I think, is this: Dwelling on remote defeaters can itself raise the level of scrutiny. Put differently, defeaters that are not salient in everyday life can be made salient simply through intensely reflecting on them. This happens to many, perhaps most, people who become seriously engaged in philosophizing. When doing philosophy, one can be made to feel the force of cartesian doubt. There are, it seems, certain philosophers who do not rise to the bait dangled by skeptical scenarios— either because they see danger in the offing or because they simply do not get it. They, perhaps, are blessed.

Why should the activity of philosophizing lead us to take cartesian skepticism seriously? Part of the reason might be that in philosophizing we are not concerned with knowledge of any particular kind. We are interested in the nature of knowledge qua knowledge. Because of this, nothing puts constraints on the range of relevant or salient defeaters. The act of philosophizing done in a certain way makes every possible defeater salient, and, with that, skepticism is inevitable. But if this diagnosis is correct, the cure seems simple enough: Don't philosophize! (At least in this way.) Unfortunately, this is not easy advice to take. Turning philosophical is not simply entering a new discipline, as changing majors is. Start anywhere and be persistent in trying to eliminate possible defeaters, and an ever-widening range of defeaters will emerge as salient. Philosophizing about knowledge arises naturally out of the enterprise of forming beliefs in the most responsible way possible. It seems unacceptable that philosophy's demand for rigor could be the source of intellectual disaster. So even though skeptical scenarios have unsolvability written on their faces, the idea persists that there must be some philosophical way to eliminate the skeptical problems they generate. I find success in this direction wholly unlikely.

Humean skepticism. The second skeptical argument we will examine comes from the writings of David Hume. It is his skeptical argument concerning induction. Hume offered this argument in a number of places, using different formulations and sometimes entangling the basic argument with other things. The clearest and briefest statement of his basic argument occurs in the *Abstract,* a short piece that Hume wrote anonymously in an (unsuccessful) effort to promote his neglected *Treatise of Human Nature,* which, he complained, had fallen "dead born" from the press.[8]

> All reasonings concerning cause and effect, are founded on experience, and . . . all reasonings from experience are founded on the supposition, that the course of nature will continue uniformly the same. We conclude, that

like causes, in like circumstances, will always produce like effects. It may now be worth while to consider, what determines us to form a conclusion of such infinite consequence.

'Tis evident, that *Adam* with all his science, would never have been able to *demonstrate,* that the course of nature must continue uniformly the same, and that the future must be conformable to the past. What is possible can never be demonstrated to be false; and 'tis possible the course of nature may change, since we can conceive such a change. Nay, I will go farther, and assert, that he could not so much as prove by any *probable* arguments, that the future must be conformable to the past. All probable arguments are built on the supposition, that there is this conformity betwixt the future and the past, and therefore can never prove it. This conformity is a *matter of fact,* and if it must be proved, will admit of no proof but from experience. But our experience in the past can be a proof of nothing for the future, but upon a supposition, that there is a resemblance betwixt them. This therefore is a point, which can admit of no proof at all, and which we take for granted without any proof.[9]

In the language of defeators, our inferences from the past to the future could be defeated if the course of nature changed, but in principle there is no way to eliminate this possibility. After all, the course of nature just might change. Though the sun has regularly risen in the past, it just might not rise tomorrow. This is certainly imaginable and is not something that can be eliminated on a priori grounds alone.[10] It seems, then, that any attempted proof that nature will continue to be uniform must be based on our experience of past uniformity, but any such proof, to work, must presuppose the very principle in question, namely, that nature is uniform. We thus arrive at a form of justification skepticism: There can be no way of justifying the principle that nature is uniform, and therefore there is no underlying justification for any inductive inferences whatsoever.

But isn't Hume merely saying that inductive inferences can never give us certainty concerning the future? No, Hume's argument supports a much stronger conclusion than that. Our belief that the patterns of future events are at least *likely* to resemble the patterns of past of events invites the same challenge: What grounds do we have for accepting this seemingly more modest proposal? Again, if the course of nature were to change, then things that occurred with reasonable likelihood in the past may simply stop happening in the future. Hume's point is that there is absolutely no way of ruling out this possibility. Hume's skeptical argument concerning induction strikes me as a perfectly unanswerable argument—unanswerable for perfectly transparent reasons. If that is right, then Quine's verdict is unavoidable: "The Humean predicament is the human predicament."[11]

Pyrrhonian skepticism. Using the distinction introduced earlier, cartesian skepticism and Humean skepticism are both examples of justification skepticism; neither is an example of belief skepticism. Perhaps with the threat of the Inquisition in mind, Descartes is careful to insist that the purely methodological character of his doubt ensures that it poses no threat to religion and morality. To this end, in the *Discourse on Method,* he adopts a moral code containing various practical maxims.

> The first was to obey the laws and customs of my country, holding constantly to the religion in which by God's grace I had been instructed from my childhood, and governing myself in all other matters according to the most moderate and least extreme opinions—the opinions commonly accepted in practice by the most sensible of those with whom I should have to live.[12]

Descartes was not a belief skeptic for another reason: He was convinced that he had adequate responses to the doubts he had raised. Hume, as we shall see in the next chapter, had quite a different reason for rejecting a thoroughgoing belief skepticism. He held, at least for many important beliefs, that it is not psychologically possible to suspend them—at least for long. In contrast, the Pyrrhonian skeptics' primary goal was to *achieve* suspension of belief, and they employed justificatory skepticism as an aid in doing so.

First, a few anecdotal remarks about the history of Pyrrhonian skepticism. Appropriately, little is known about the founder of this movement, Pyrrho of Ellis (360–270 B.C.). As the story goes, Pyrrho, behaving in a typically Greek way, was attempting to understand the underlying nature of the universe and our place in it. By chance, one day he found himself in a position where the reasons for and the reasons against the philosophical theses that concerned him were exactly in balance and thus canceled each other out. This resulted in a total suspension of belief on these philosophical matters. Finding himself in this state, he further discovered to his surprise that he felt good! Indeed, the peace of mind that swept over him when he reached this neutral state amounted to blessedness. With this accidental discovery—and it is important that it was an accidental discovery—a new style of philosophizing was born. Instead of trying to resolve philosophical questions concerning the nature of the universe and one's place in it, the aim was to attain complete neutrality on such matters in order to attain the blessedness that, as it turns out, such a neutral state brings. Thus the aim of this new way of philosophizing was to eliminate rather than to establish philosophical commitments.

There is little reason to think that this charming story is literally true, but symbolically it captures the essence of Pyrrhonism. Pyrrhonism is a philosophy with a practical aim: the blessedness achieved by curing oneself of philosophical commitments. It also provides a therapeutic method intended to bring about this result. The early Pyrrhonists employed the method of equipolence, or balancing, as a way of achieving suspension of belief. Anytime they found themselves inclined to one side of a philosophical issue, they would attempt to find equally strong reasons supporting its opposite side. Perhaps because this is rather hard work, the later Pyrrhonists found more-general procedures for attaining suspension of belief. These procedures were collected and explained by Sextus Empiricus (c. A.D. 200) in his *Outlines of Pyrrhonism* and in a series of *Against* works: *Against the Logicians*, *Against the Mathematicians*, *Against the Grammarians*, *Against the Professors*, and so on.[13]

We can get a sense of Pyrrhonian skepticism by contrasting it with cartesian skepticism. A central difference between cartesian skepticism and traditional Pyrrhonian skepticism is that cartesian skepticism, but not Pyrrhonian skepticism, explicitly denies that certain kinds of knowledge are possible. For example, taking claims to perceptual knowledge as their target, the cartesian skeptic typically presents arguments purporting to show that perception cannot provide us with any knowledge of the world around us because we are in no way able to meet the challenges presented by skeptical scenarios. The Pyrrhonian skeptic makes no such claim, for, though various challenges to the reliability of the senses are possible, by themselves they do not show that reliable empirical knowledge can *never* be attained. Showing that would demand an argument much stronger than one a Pyrrhonian skeptic would be willing to employ. For the Pyrrhonian skeptics, the claim that a certain kind of knowledge is impossible amounts to *negative dogmatism,* a charge they brought against their ancient rivals the Academic skeptics. The Pyrrhonian skeptics simply report how things strike them, saying, perhaps, that for all they know we can have no empirical knowledge and for all they know we can have empirical knowledge. On this matter they find themselves in a position where they can say nothing more—"nothing more" being one of their favorite tag phrases. The Pyrrhonian skeptic does not dogmatize on this or on any other matter.

A second difference between cartesian skepticism and Pyrrhonian skepticism concerns the target of the skeptical attack. The cartesian (that is, skeptical-scenario) skeptic raises doubts that call into question all empirical knowledge—including our most common beliefs about the world around us. If I am in a vat on a planet circling Alpha Centuri and am wired so that all I seem to see about me is nothing but a dream induced in me by a demon, then I do not know—as I think I know—that I am revising this chapter at the Ligurian Study Center in Bogliasco, Italy. For the cartesian skeptic, if an adequate response to this skeptical scenario is not forthcoming, I am then obliged to reject even my most common, ordinary claims to knowledge. In contrast—though this is a disputed point—the Pyrrhonian skeptic does not target common, everyday beliefs for skeptical assault. The primary target of Pyrrhonian skepticism is dogmatic philosophy, with occasional sallies into other fields where dogmatizing of a similar kind takes place. The attacks of the Pyrrhonian skeptic are directed against the dogmas of "professors," not against the beliefs of common people pursuing the honest (or even dishonest) business of daily life. Furthermore, nothing that the Pyrrhonian skeptic says leads to a skeptical critique of common belief. Properly understood, the Pyrrhonian skeptic's attack on the dogmatic beliefs of the professors does not carry over to common beliefs that are unpretentiously held.[14]

To test this claim that the Pyrrhonian skeptic does not dogmatize, we can consider perhaps the best-known maneuver in the Pyrrhonian corpus, the treatment of the criterion of truth. The Stoic epistemologists held that to judge correctly, one must be in possession of a proper criterion of truth—a test that provides invincible evidence for the truth of some belief. Presented with such a claim, the Pyrrhonian skeptic proceeds hypothetically by assuming that the dogmatist is correct in demanding a correct criterion of truth and then draws out the consequences of this demand. The Pyrrhonist presents his dogmatic opponent with the following argument: If someone presents a criterion of truth, then it will be important to determine whether it is the *correct* criterion. There is, after all, disagreement concerning which, if any, criterion is the correct criterion of truth. If the stated criterion is said to be correct without the employment of a criterion of truth, then, on their own principles, the dogmatists are defeated. If the criterion is defended on the basis of a criterion of truth, then it must either be the same criterion or a different one. If the same criterion of truth is used for judging the criterion of truth, then the defense of the criterion will be question-begging. If a new criterion of truth is used, then the challenge is repeated, ad infinitum if necessary. Thus, the dual demons of circularity and infinite regress are let loose as soon as the Stoics attempt to defend their choice of a criterion of truth. If they refuse to defend it, then they have simply abandoned their idea that all judgments must be made in conformity with a correct criterion of truth.[15]

This account of the argument concerning the criterion of truth embodies—though in a condensed form—what Sextus called the Five Modes leading to the suspension of belief, attributed by him to the later Pyrrhonist Agrippa. Sextus describes the Five Modes in these words:

The later Sceptics laid down Five Modes leading to suspension [of belief], namely these: the first based on discrepancy, the second on regress *ad infinitum,* the third on relativity, the fourth on hypothesis, the fifth on circular reasoning.[16]

One way of viewing the Five Modes is to divide them into two groups. Discrepancy and relativity both point to disparities in belief and thus call for reasons for accepting one belief over its competitors. Discrepancy simply means that different people have different opinions about various matters and we therefore need some way of choosing between them. Relativity means that a thing can appear differently depending on who is perceiving it, the state of the perceiver, the perceptual setting, and so forth. We are then challenged to produce a good reason for accepting one appearance rather than the others.[17] The remaining three modes, regress ad infinitum, hypothesis (mere unjustified assertion), and circularity, set a dialectical trap for anyone who attempts to meet the demand for complete justification. There seems to be no way of avoiding either arguing endlessly, arguing in a circle, or abandoning argument altogether.

The discussion of the criterion of truth gives a brief illustration of the Five Modes at work, but it is important to see that they can be applied to any dogmatic claim whatsoever. They provide a recipe for a completely general form of philosophical skepticism. Suppose the dogmatist in question is Democritus, who held that the universe is nothing more than a system of indestructible atoms moving about through an otherwise empty space. This is a matter that has been disputed by others, so we need to be given adequate reasons for accepting his view rather than accepting one of its competitors. The reasons will themselves now be interrogated and the dialectical trap involving circularity, infinite regress, or unjustified assertion sprung. This procedure can be employed anytime, with any dogmatic assertion that anyone makes.

But at this point, hasn't it become evident—despite their disclaimers—that by invoking the Five Modes the Pyrrhonian skeptics are themselves dogmatizing?[18] As Sextus Empiricus repeatedly insists, the answer to this question is no. The demands presented in the Five Modes belong to the dogmatists themselves, that is, they formulate criteria of adequacy that dogmatists accept as governing their enterprise. The Pyrrhonist is not committed to any such intellectual ideal. The Pyrrhonian skeptic adopts the dogmatists' stance only to show the dogmatists that their efforts are inadequate by their own standards. That done, the Pyrrhonian skeptic discharges the Five Modes—as it were, discards them as a ladder no longer needed or, more dramatically, flushes them out, along with the dogmatic beliefs they were intended to undermine.[19] Sextus, who it seems was a physician, compares this procedure to the use of an aperient drug.

> For, in regard to all the Sceptic expressions, we must grasp first the fact that we make no positive assertion respecting their absolute truth, since we say that they may possibly be confuted by themselves, seeing that

they themselves are included in the things to which their doubt applies, just as aperient drugs do not merely eliminate the humours from the body, but also expel themselves along with the humours.[20]

Though this is not always recognized, the Five Modes are an implicit, but potent, force on the contemporary philosophical scene. Many contemporary epistemologists set themselves the task of responding to Agrippa's Five Modes, whether they know them by this name or not. The following passage from Laurence BonJour is a typical example of an epistemologist's willingness to take the Agrippa problem head on:

> *Prima facie,* there are four main logical possibilities as to the eventual outcome of the potential regress of epistemic justification. . . . (1) The regress might terminate with beliefs . . . for which no justification of any kind [is given]. . . . (2) The regress might continue indefinitely "backwards." . . . (3) The regress might circle back upon itself. . . . (4) The regress might terminate because "basic" empirical beliefs are reached.[21]

This is essentially Agrippa's Five Modes with the two "starter" modes, discrepancy and relativity, dropped and the foundationalist alternative (option 4) added.

Because option 1 seems to give the show away to the skeptic and option 2 seems unattractive in burdening us with an unending task, until relatively recently the battle has been fought between those who take one of the last two options.[22] Coherentists take the third option, arguing that if the circle is big enough, rich enough, coherent enough, and so on, then there is nothing wrong with circularity. Foundationalists hold that there are certain propositions that can justifiably be accepted without appeal to other propositions to support them. In *Pyrrhonian Reflections on Knowledge and Justification,* I pose the following question: How well do either coherentists or foundationalists do in solving the Agrippa problem if Agrippa is made a party to the dispute? After examining what I take to be the strongest candidates for the solution to the problem of empirical knowledge (or empirical justification), I arrive at the conclusion that, as far as I can see, things are now largely where Sextus left them almost two thousand years ago.

There is, however, something disappointing (in some ways boring) about the traditional Pyrrhonian technique of criticism: Though it provides deadly weaponry for undermining philosophical commitments taken on their own terms, it gives no account, or at least no insightful account, of the sources of philosophical commitments themselves. We want to understand these as well. To return to the medical analogy, we want a pathology that helps us understand the disease and not only a therapy for curing it. The notion of rising levels of scrutiny introduced earlier seems to provide the key for understanding the source of epistemological perplexities. Here I will look at this notion in more detail.

The following seems to be true: In everyday life, we often claim to know things with little sense that we are engaged in something special or doing something especially difficult. The word "know" is not a term restricted to philosophy any more than the words "good" and "true" are. Yet when we philosophize—in Barry Stroud's phrase, when we commit epistemology—we typically encounter difficulties. Cartesian skepticism is one such difficulty. Humean skepticism is another. Pyrrhonian skepticism is a third. This naturally raises the following question: What is it about the ordinary concept of knowledge, and what is it about the enterprise of doing epistemology that yield these difficulties?

We can begin by noting commonplaces (platitudes) concerning knowledge claims. There is general agreement that for someone, usually called S, to know that p, S must believe that p and this belief must be true. (I do not think the belief clause is altogether unproblematic, but I won't go into that here.) Since the appearance of Plato's *Theaetetus* almost two and a half millennia ago, it has also been generally granted that there must be more to knowledge than this. As it stands, this account of knowledge would lead us to attribute knowledge to someone who believes something that happens to be true but does so on unsound grounds or on no grounds whatsoever. A person might, for example, believe that a horse will win a race for no other reason than it is gray. If that horse does win, we will hardly credit him with knowing that it would, for he had no sound reason for believing this. If that is the problem, then the solution seems easy enough: We can simply add the further restriction that S believe that p on grounds or reasons that are sound.

The serious business of doing epistemology usually begins by challenging the adequacy of various versions of this additional clause. It can seem too strong in some ways, too weak in others. In fact, I think that this is just the right thing to say. The difficulty, however, is to calm down about the notions of sound reasons or sound grounds. Under what conditions are grounds or reasons taken to be sound? With respect to everyday knowledge claims, the answer seems to be this: Through our upbringing and education, we acquire certain justificatory techniques or justificatory procedures. Sometimes these techniques involve the direct use of our senses. One way to be sure of something is to go look for yourself. Other justificatory procedures can be more complex—some extraordinarily complex. Furthermore, human beings have the capacity to encode information into propositions and then use these propositions as reasons supporting other propositions. Using such a justificatory procedure is called presenting an argument; when suitably rigorous, such arguments are called proofs or demonstrations. The function of a justificatory procedure, whether simple or complex, is to rule out possible defeaters to a knowledge claim. Thus, to believe something on grounds or reasons that are sound involves accepting it, using the appropriate justificatory procedure.

To repeat a point made briefly earlier, one important feature of justificatory procedures—from the simplest to the most complex—is that they contain mechanisms that heighten the level of scrutiny. In acquiring justificatory procedures we also learn to recognize when more care than usual is needed in applying them. When trying to match colors, it is often necessary to examine them in daylight. If you don't do this, then you cannot tell (hence do not know) whether they match or not. To cite a famous example, normally it is sufficient to identify something as a barn simply by observing it from the road. However, if we are given the additional information that most of the structures along the road are mere barn facsimiles, then we realize that the standard procedure of just looking is not adequate for identifying something as a barn.[23] In somewhat technical language, the discovery of certain facts can trigger a higher level of scrutiny that widens the range of possible defeators.

An important feature of our ordinary justificatory practices is that levels of scrutiny are triggered by the discovery of certain facts that show us that ordinary levels of caution are no longer fully adequate. We then hitch up the level of scrutiny in standard ways. Of course, some people are more punctilious than others are; they are more cautious in their knowledge claims than others. As we say, they are pickier. In fact, we possess a rather rich vocabulary of signals concerning levels of scrutiny. In a conversation, for example, we are expected to adopt the ongoing level of scrutiny, signaling shifts in the levels of scrutiny when we make them. If we want to operate at a lower level of scrutiny than is really demanded, we can signal this by using such words and phrases as "perhaps," "I wouldn't be surprised if," "ballpark figure," and the like. There are also standard signals for raising the level of scrutiny, for example "This may not seem immediately relevant, but . . ." Developing an account of the rules governing levels of scrutiny would, I think, be a profitable activity.[24] I cannot go into this very far here, but one such maxim would be this: Do not raise the level of scrutiny in the absence of a particular reason that triggers it. One main trigger is the recognition that the setting is nonstandard in some relevant way; another concerns the importance of getting things right. We sensibly take more care in life-or-death matters. In fancy language, raising the level of scrutiny involves *epistemic transaction costs* that, like most costs, we prefer not to incur.

We can now turn our attention to the philosopher who engages in epistemology along traditional lines. My suggestion is that traditional epistemology is driven and shaped by persistent violations of the maxim just cited. Philosophers—though not all of them—raise the level of scrutiny through reflection alone. In fact, most people can be induced into doing this to some extent just by reflecting intensely on defeasible but undefeated defeaters. I'll try. Do you really know who your parents are? For most people the answer seems to be yes. But many adopted children are never apprised of this fact about them. Not only that, babies sometimes get switched in hospitals. Now there are ways of eliminating these possibilities, for example, using DNA testing, but few people have even thought of doing this. Reflecting on cases of this kind, can you really claim to know who your parents are? If this little exercise has kicked you into a higher level of scrutiny, you will be strongly inclined to say, "Well, no, strictly speaking, I do not really know who my parents are." It is interesting how many people succumb to this temptation in a philosophy classroom. It is also interesting how quickly it vanishes outside the classroom when scrutiny subsides to its normal, more relaxed level.

It has often been argued that skeptics themselves are responsible for skepticism because they impose arbitrarily high standards for knowledge. That gets the story wrong. If what has been said here is broadly correct, then skepticism is not the result of an arbitrary imposition, but instead grows naturally out of the epistemological project itself. That is the point of the passage from Hume cited at the head of this chapter:

> As the sceptical doubt arises naturally from a profound and intense reflection on [epistemology], it always encreases the farther we carry our reflections, whether in opposition or conformity to it.

We have seen three instances of this. The first was cartesian skepticism with its demand that we eliminate wildly remote (perhaps in principle uneliminable) defeators. The second involved Hume's challenge that we find some non-question-begging way of ruling out the possibility that the course of nature might change. The third and perhaps most difficult challenge is to find some way of dealing with the general skeptical implications generated by Agrippa's Five Modes. If we work our way into a position where we take the Agrippa problem seriously—as many philosophers have—it will, it seems, prove quite impossible to solve. Unrestricted philosophizing itself generates all these skeptical challenges and, as it seems, meets none of them. How in fact skepticism is avoided—to the extent that it *is* avoided—is the topic of the next chapter.

It is necessary that a method should be found by which our beliefs be determined by nothing human, but by some external permanency—by something upon which our thinking has no effect.

C. S. Peirce, "The Fixation of Belief"

If we see knowing not as having an essence, to be described by scientists or philosophers, but rather as a right, by current standards, to believe, then we are well on the way to seeing *conversation* as the ultimate context within which knowledge is to be understood.

Richard Rorty, *Philosophy and the Mirror of Nature*

CHAPTER FIVE

Modest Responses to These Challenges

If we look back at the previous three chapters, things seem to be becoming "worser and worser." According to the second chapter, the rules that govern our thought and action are pervasively prone to inconsistency—an inconsistency that may not ever be eliminable in a fully acceptable way. In the third chapter we saw, following Kant, that our rational faculties, when given unlimited freedom, generate dialectical illusions that yield irresolvable conflicts. Finally, in the previous chapter we saw how our critical faculties, when unrestrained, can lead us into forlorn skepticism.

There is a thread that runs through all these cases: the detachment of the intellectual from all nonintellectual controlling constraints. The image of this difficulty is beautifully captured by Kant's metaphor of the dove complaining about the air resistance slowing its flight. It is also captured in the passage cited above in which C. S. Peirce tells us, "It is necessary that a method should be found by which our beliefs be determined by nothing human." This means that our conceptual activities can avoid disaster only if they are constrained by something nonconceptual. The reverse attitude, that this cannot be done, is captured in the passage from Richard Rorty. In this chapter we will examine ways in which nonconceptual constraints might function. We will begin with skeptical challenges.

If the skeptical arguments examined in the previous chapter are correct, aren't we forced, in Hume's words, to "reject all belief and reasoning, and . . . look upon no opinion even as more probable or likely than another"?[1] At the very least, aren't we being dishonest—aren't we in intellectual bad faith—if we don't? Hume's remarkable answer is that the standpoint of radical skepticism is not, except under strained and artificial circumstances, an option open to us. Skeptical doubts, he tells us, are not sustainable outside our studies. In the *Treatise of Human Nature* Hume puts it this way:

> Most fortunately it happens, that since reason is incapable of dispelling these clouds, nature herself suffices to that purpose, and cures me of this philosophical melancholy and delirium, either by relaxing this bent of mind, or by some avocation, and lively impression of my senses, which obliterate all these chimeras. I dine, I play

a game of back-gammon, I converse, and am merry with
my friends; and when after three or four hours' amuse-
ment, I wou'd return to these speculations, they appear
so cold, and strain'd, and ridiculous, that I cannot find
in my heart to enter into them any farther.[2]

It is important to understand clearly what Hume is
saying. In this passage he is not putting forward any
argument, even a pragmatic argument, in response to the
skeptical arguments he has previously presented. He is
making no effort to *refute* skepticism. He is simply reporting
facts as he sees them: Skeptical doubts that overwhelm us
when we are engaged in intense philosophical reflection
largely fade when we are engaged in the everyday business
or the everyday pleasures of life. In the fifth section of his
Enquiry Concerning Human Understanding, Hume labels this
response to skepticism, rather oddly, a "skeptical solution"
to these doubts. By this I think he means a solution that
does not deny the soundness of skeptical arguments but,
instead, merely points out their inefficacy in controlling our
beliefs in anything but the hothouse setting of wholly
unfettered reflection.

In the *Enquiry Concerning Human Understanding,* Hume
produces a response to his skeptical worries that is richer
than the one found in his *Treatise.* Hume observes that,
despite our lack of rational grounds for doing so, human
beings do in fact project past regularities into the future.
He asks how this could be. His answer is that we are so
constructed that the experience of past regularities conditions us to make such projections. Where we speak of

conditioning, Hume speaks of custom and habit, but the underlying notion is the same. The crucial point is that skeptical problems generated by reflection are overcome by our entering into causal relations with the world around us. With a certain tone of mockery, Hume makes the point this way:

> Here, then, is a kind of pre-established harmony between the course of nature and the succession of our ideas; and though the powers and forces, by which the former is governed, be wholly unknown to us; yet our thoughts and conceptions have still, we find, gone on in the same train with the other works of nature. Custom is that principle, by which this correspondence has been effected; so necessary to the subsistence of our species, and the regulation of our conduct, in every circumstance and occurrence of human life. Had not the presence of an object instantly excited the idea of those objects, commonly conjoined with it, all our knowledge must have been limited to the narrow sphere of our memory and senses; and we should never have been able to adjust means to ends, or employ our natural powers, either to the producing of good, or avoiding of evil. Those, who delight in the discovery and contemplation of *final causes,* have here ample subject to employ their wonder and admiration.[3]

The mockery involves the use of the notions of preestablished harmony and final causes—both of which Hume considers features of outdated metaphysics.

Beyond the mockery, Hume is, I think, saying something of fundamental importance. In this passage (and throughout his writings) Hume treats human beings as *natural* creatures standing in causal relationships with other objects in nature. We are the kind of creatures we are—for example, we hold the fundamental beliefs that we do—because we enter into these causal relations. When we enter into these causal relationships with the world, for example, through perception, certain beliefs are forced on us. To see this, look at your hand and try by an act of will to believe that it is not a hand you are seeing but an ear of corn instead. In this case, believing and withholding belief are not matters under our direct control. If Hume is right, the same constraints hold for many of our beliefs about the future. With a candle before you, you can *imagine* that putting your hand in it will not cause pain, but is this something that you can genuinely *believe?* Hume's answer is no. Given our past experience with fire, we automatically expect to feel pain if we come in contact with it. This relationship is more primitive than thinking. Without mentioning him by name, Wittgenstein gets Hume's standpoint exactly right when he says:

> 472. The character of the belief in the uniformity of nature can perhaps be seen most clearly in the case in which we fear what we expect. Nothing could induce me to put my hand into a flame—although after all it is *only in the past* that I have burnt myself.
> 473. The belief that fire will burn me is of the same kind as the fear that it will burn me.[4]

Here we have the picture of nature bringing our ideas into tune with it, rather than us intellectually attuning our thoughts to nature.

Though it points us in the right direction, I do not find Hume's "skeptical" response to skepticism fully satisfactory. It may be comforting to be told that beliefs formed and sustained through immersion in the natural order will be immune to skeptical doubt. In dealing with the natural world, we must modestly take the part of second fiddle.

> In general, there is a degree of doubt, and caution, and modesty, which, in all kinds of scrutiny and decision, ought for ever to accompany a just reasoner.[5]

Hume's writings show us the abyss that opens if we abandon such modesty. But precisely how modest should we be? Hume thought we should be very modest indeed. Passages of the following kind are found throughout his writings:

> It must certainly be allowed, that nature has kept us at a great distance from all her secrets, and has afforded us only the knowledge of a few superficial qualities of objects; while she conceals from us those powers and principles on which the influence of these objects entirely depends. Our senses inform us of the colour, weight, and consistence of bread; but neither sense nor reason *can ever inform us* of those qualities which fit it for the nourishment and support of a human body.[6]

By advocating intellectual modesty, Hume is not suggesting that we abandon philosophizing altogether, but he is insisting that those who recognize the standing threat of skepticism will place strong constraints on the range of issues they will attempt to pursue.

> Those who have a propensity to philosophy, will still continue their researches; because they reflect, that, besides the immediate pleasure, attending such an occupation, philosophical decisions are nothing but the reflections of common life, methodized and corrected. But they will never be tempted to go beyond common life, so long as they consider the imperfection of those faculties which they employ, their narrow reach, and their inaccurate operations.[7]

Though Hume's insistence on modesty in our intellectual activities has the ring of cautious good sense, it suffers from a fundamental defect. It runs counter to an undeniable historical fact. Over the past four centuries there have been extraordinary developments in the natural sciences—developments that simply falsify Hume's predictions concerning what we as human beings are capable of knowing. We do, despite Hume's pessimistic forecasts, now possess a tolerably good understanding of how bread nourishes, and our knowledge extends to matters much more esoteric than this. If Hume's assessment of human intellectual capacities were correct, then the Scientific Revolution could not have taken place. But it did, so there is something wrong with Hume's assessment of the powers of the human mind.

Our basic question, then, is this: Given all our intellectual liabilities—including seemingly unanswerable skeptical arguments—how are we to account for the undoubted advances in science?

One answer makes quick work of this question: There have been no advances in science, so there are no advances to account for. Employing yet another version of perspectivism, it has been fashionable in some circles to dismiss the claim that science has made genuine progress. Successive scientific theories, it is suggested, are simply different forms of discourse, which, being incommensurable, admit of no ranking, either among themselves or with respect to other forms of discourse. Views of this kind were encouraged by some incautious statements found in the first edition of Thomas Kuhn's pathbreaking work *The Structure of Scientific Revolutions* about the incommensurability of scientific frameworks. They get their strongest expression in hyperbolic outbursts that Paul Feyerabend sometimes finds irresistible. Here are some samples from Feyerabend's notorious book *Against Method:*

> Chinese technology for a long time lacked any Western-scientific underpinning, and yet it was far ahead of contemporary Western technology. It is true that Western science now reigns supreme all over the globe; however, the reason was not insight in its "inherent rationality" but power play (the colonizing nations imposed their way of living) and the need for weapons: Western science so far has created the most efficient instruments of death.[8]

Famously:

> There is only one principle that can be defended under
> *all* circumstances and in all stages of human develop-
> ment. It is the principle: anything goes.[9]

In discussing the acceptance of Galileo's cosmology, he tells
us:

> Theories become clear and "reasonable" only *after*
> incoherent parts of them have been used for a long
> time.[10]

As an example of thumbing one's nose at the demand that
the conceptual must be constrained by something that is
not conceptual, it is hard to beat the following.

> A scientist who is interested in maximal empirical
> content, and who wants to understand as many aspects
> of his theory as possible, will adopt a pluralistic meth-
> odology. He will compare theories with other theories
> rather than with "experience," "data," or "facts," and
> will try to improve rather than discard the views that
> appear to lose in the competition.[11]

Feyerabend and Rorty (at least in the passage quoted at
the start of this chapter) strike me as a specimens of a
philosophers fully captured by dialectical illusions of perspectivism or relativity—though both, on occasion, engage
in tactical backtracking. To the extent that these writers stick

to their radical guns, their standpoints suffer from the same defect that Hume's does: They fail to make sense out of the undoubted achievements in science-driven technology.

Let me explain what I mean by the phrase "science-driven technology." For a long period of human history, technological advances were made independent of and usually prior to scientific understanding. Alloys were discovered and perfected thousands of years before a theory emerged that could explain them. Telescopes and microscopes were constructed before there was an adequate science of optics. Mere "mechanics," to use Francis Bacon's phrase, made progress in developing practical mechanisms, while those who pursued science with clean hands produced merely chatter. Bacon thought there was an important lesson to be learned from this disparity between progress in the mechanical arts and a lack of progress in purely intellectual spheres. The following marvelous passage is worth quoting at length:

> It must be plainly avowed that that wisdom which we have derived principally from the Greeks is but like the boyhood of knowledge, and has the characteristic property of boys: it can talk, but it cannot generate; for it is fruitful of controversies but barren of works. . . . Observe also, that if sciences of this kind had any life in them, that could never have come to pass which has been the case now for many ages—that they stand almost at a stay, without receiving any augmentations worthy of the human race; insomuch that many times not only what was asserted once is asserted still, but what

was a question once is a question still. . . . In the
mechanical arts we do not find it so; they, on the
contrary, as having in them some breath of life, are
continually growing and becoming more perfect. As
originally invented they are commonly rude, clumsy,
and shapeless; afterwards they acquire new powers and
more commodious arrangements and constructions
. . . . Philosophy and the intellectual sciences, on the
contrary, stand like statues, worshipped and celebrated,
but not moved or advanced.[12]

The success of technology *prior* to the success of science
here observed by Bacon provides a clue to answering our
basic question: What is it that provides a check against our
thought? What is the nonconceptual element or noninter-
pretive element that prevents our thought from turning
either skeptical or dialectical? With technology, the answer
is usually straightforward. If you build a mechanism to do
something—to produce a laser beam or to put string
handles on shopping bags—and it doesn't work, then there
is something wrong with the mechanism. Excuses can be
made up to point: The mechanism wasn't assembled
properly. It is out of adjustment. It needs oil. Sometimes
excuses of this kind turn out to be legitimate, but usually
after a short period such excuses are no longer tolerated.
We are forced to say that the design—that is, the idea, the
thought behind the mechanism, the conception that generated it—is in some way mistaken. Here reality confronts
thought in just the uncompromising way that Peirce
envisaged. Whether the Big Bang theory is correct will

probably be discussed for decades; that the Hubble telescope, when first put into space, was not focusing correctly
was settled in short order. The problem with the Hubble
telescope illustrates what it is like to encounter reality—to
be constrained by it. When the instrument was ailing,
nobody suggested that it took a telescope as powerful as the
Hubble to show how fuzzy stars really are. There are certain
things that you can't talk your way out of—where learning
jargon doesn't help.

Francis Bacon also saw that coming to understand
nature involved intervening in it, telling us that "the secrets
of nature reveal themselves more readily under the vexa-
tions of art than when they go their own way."[13] On this
view, an experiment is a way of extracting information
from nature by, as it were, putting it on the rack. But the
reverse emphasis is equally important: Performing experiments is a way of putting our beliefs, partially at least, into
the hands of nature. An experiment is not a conversation
with nature, for nature is both deaf and mute. With an
experiment, we make up our minds—perhaps change our
minds—because things have happened one way rather than
another. Experiments are not clumsy substitutes for
thought experiments.

Furthermore, a piece of scientific apparatus is not
simply a mechanism for gathering observations for testing
theories. The very possibility of producing a mechanism
of a certain kind often depends on the prior establishment
of scientific theories. When a mechanism produced under
the guidance of such a theory actually works more or less
as it is supposed to, this can provide strong confirmation

of the theory used to design it. The mechanism can also provide the basis for further scientific discoveries. Consider the linear accelerator. A linear accelerator is a theory-inspired mechanism. If a certain theory is broadly correct, then it should be possible to construct a mechanism that will accelerate particles in certain ways. The mechanism is produced and, perhaps with some interesting surprises, works pretty much the way it should. With luck, this mechanism then produces a new range of data that provides the basis for further scientific advances, including the development of new linear accelerators. It is in this way that theoretical science and technology interpenetrate and indeed saturate one another.

It can also happen that a mechanism is constructed under the guidance of a well-established theory and then doesn't behave in the way it is supposed to. If the theory is deeply entrenched, this may lead to efforts to adjust the machine so that it works "correctly." Considerable time and money might be spent in doing this, but if in the end the mechanism refuses to behave the way it is supposed to, then it is the theory that inspired it, not the mechanism, that needs adjusting.

I hope all this sounds platitudinous, but it is worth dwelling on because it provides a clear example of concepts being constrained by something that is not itself conceptual. But even this may be challenged on the ground that it is simply circular. Under the guidance of a theory we construct a mechanism and then—"surprise, surprise," someone might say—declare the theory confirmed when the mechanism functions as the theory predicts. Feyerabend seems to be saying something like this in the following passage:

> *Measuring instruments* are constructed in accordance with laws and their readings are tested under the assumption that these laws are correct.[14]

But the charge of circularity is wholly misplaced: It ignores the fact that when the mechanism is constructed, *it may not work the way it is supposed to or may not work at all.* Circularity arises only when the theory is used to explain away any failure come what may. When this happens, thought has again turned merely dialectical and the connection with the world has been severed.

Our problem was this: Given the presence of seemingly unanswerable skeptical problems and also the tendency of the human mind to turn dialectical, we have been trying to find some explanation of the undoubted progress of science. The answer, fully spelled out, will involve two components. The first is the Humean component mentioned earlier, allowing our ideas to be caused by nonrational factors. This is a way of avoiding maladies generated by the unrestricted use of reason, but it still leaves unexplained the positive developments of science. The second component involves, in one way or another, breaking down the barrier between thought and the world by embodying thought in objects. It involves intervening in the world and becoming causally entangled with it—having our beliefs arise because of this entanglement. This can involve no more than using a piece of wood to prevent a door from being blown open by the wind. If the door still blows open, this shows that the thought embodied in using this chunk of the world in the way we did was false. This mind-world interaction is a constant feature of our daily lives. It finds its richest expression in the two-way movement of science-driven technology and technology-driven science.

It is always possible to hang on to a belief or refuse to accept a belief no matter what happens. There is no upper limit to ad hoc excuses. In common parlance this is called being pigheaded. A fancier way of referring to something as pigheaded is to say that it is being maintained in a self-sealing way. A position is self-sealing if it is set up in such way that experience, however it turns out, cannot possibly bear against it. One reason that science and technology have advanced is that their practitioners have adopted a policy of relatively low tolerance for pigheadedness—for self-sealing moves. Antipigheadedness is part of the intellectual culture of science. I say *relatively* low, because pigheaded-ness is a human trait and scientists are human beings. Think of the resistance to large-scale innovations of Copernicus, Galileo, Darwin, and Einstein. But pigheadedness is hard to maintain in technology, because a machine that does not work is fairly quickly discarded. The same is true of all sciences with a rich operational component. When we deal with highly abstract cosmologies—string theory and the like—then testing becomes only a remote possibility and a wide range of alternative answers opens up, with seemingly no way of adjudicating among them. At times things begin to look suspiciously dialectical. Here many scientists them-selves become worried, as they should.

Scientists are, in general, pickier than most people—at least when engaged in scientific activity—but science depends on placing limits on pickiness. Certain possibilities, though checkable, are considered too remote or too far-fetched to be worth spending time on. This is not laziness but good scientific husbandry. It rests on the assumption that if something important is ignored or misunderstood, it will sooner or later intrude itself into an experimental setting. Because scientists do not concern themselves with far-fetched possibilities, they do not find it mandatory to respond to skeptical scenarios before commencing their research. It is sometimes said that scientists have an obligation (which they typically shirk) to establish the legitimacy of science as a whole. This, however, amounts to asking the scientist to abandon the nonconceptual constraints that protect science from becoming merely dialectical—to abandon science as Peirce conceives it in favor of science as Feyerabend and Rorty conceive it.

What about our first worry, that human systems of thought are pervasively paradox-prone? It doesn't seem to me that science can fully avoid this problem. Paradox seems concomitant with increasing complexity of thought, and because the world, evidently, is a complex structure, the systems used to represent it will be complex as well. Yet there is this solace: As we saw in the first chapter, the world may be so complex that its structures are computationally inaccessible; it may contain objective indeterminacies; it may exhibit features that, from a commonsense standpoint, are literally unimaginable; and so on; but it cannot itself embody contradictions. To think otherwise is simply to misunderstand what a contradiction is. To the extent, then, that thought can find embodiment in mechanisms, instruments, and the like, to that extent the threat of paradox has been reduced.

At this point we can hear the voice of the critic declaring, "How does any of this help? Specifically, until skepticism is refuted, isn't all of this talk about making thought concrete in mechanisms simply question-begging? Maybe you just are a brain in a vat. If so, you have no right to speak in a naive way about intervening in the world and learning from these interventions. If the course of nature might change, then how mechanisms work now will provide no sure guide to their operation in the future." This criticism misrepresents the aim of our discussion, which is not an attempt to refute skepticism. It is intended to be no more than what Hume calls a "skeptical solution." It concedes that thought, when it proceeds in a certain way, is self-destructive in the related ways of falling into paradox, of turning dialectical or becoming skeptical. My view is that when problems arise in this way, they are completely intelligible and wholly unanswerable. The question here is factual: What in science and ordinary life blocks this drift into intellectual disaster? In the *Treatise* Hume's answer relies on the weakness of the human mind:

> We save ourselves from this total scepticism only by means of that singular and seemingly trivial property of the fancy, by which we enter with difficulty into remote views of things, and are not able to accompany them with so sensible an impression, as we do those, which are more easy and natural.[15]

On this diagnosis, if our faculties were stronger, we would be prepared to believe even less.

In the *Enquiry,* as we saw, Hume makes the more generous suggestion that we are saved from skepticism by the way in which our belief-formation mechanisms are tuned to the world. Provided that we do not distort these mechanisms by intense reflection, nature will produce in us beliefs in regularities that match—at least well enough— regularities in nature itself. The idea that technology coalesces world and mind is a similar view, with the difference that the mind is a more nearly equal—though still subservient—partner in the transaction.

But suppose we are brains in vats, or the course of nature will change? There is nothing to be done about that.

CHAPTER SIX

Matters of Taste

De gustibus non est disputandum. (There is no disputing matters of taste.)

Origin interestingly obscure[1]

Fashions fade, style is eternal.

Yves Saint Laurent

In the previous chapter I claimed that the excesses of reason can be curbed in the natural sciences by embedding thought in the world, for example, in mechanisms and instruments of various kinds. With a mechanism, the divorce between theory and practice is annulled. A mechanism is, in this sense, a concrete universal. Here, I am sure, someone will complain that all this may be well and good for the natural sciences, where help is hardly needed anyway, but that it seems to have no application to disciplines in the humanities. Am I suggesting that the humanities adopt the methods of experimental science? Am I suggesting that these disciplines will be shown to be otiose or frivolous if they cannot do this? No to both questions. We do have a right to ask how a discipline—criticism, for example—solves the resistance problem; that is, how its concepts are constrained by something nonconceptual. We have, however, no right to place antecedent constraints on how this is to be done.

In the passages cited above, we again hear the competing voices of two radically opposed positions. The first, "De gustibus" et cetera, is simply the Protagorean principle that man is the measure of all things applied to matters of taste and aesthetic judgment. The second, with its contrast between the transience of fashion and the eternality of style, could hardly be more Parmenidean. For Saint Laurent, himself a fashion designer, adherents to the *de gustibus* principle, if I may call it that, dwell only in the realm of various fleeting images of style without grasping the underlying conception itself. His Protagorean opponents, in turn, will dismiss such talk, to borrow a phrase from Jeremy Bentham, as "nonsense on stilts."

Each standpoint has its difficulties. Saying "It is all just a matter of taste" is an all-purpose stopper of discussions of aesthetic values. It can be uttered at any time with respect to any work of art or literature. More importantly, it completely severs the connection with the actual properties of the object under consideration. In this respect, it functions much like another all-purpose stopper: "Yeah, that's what you say." In both cases, all material considerations are marginalized, and content has been drained from the discussion. Perhaps surprisingly, a similar loss of content occurs when Saint Laurent appeals to style as something distinct from fashion. Presumably the work of some fashion designers better exemplifies style than the work of others, but being told that one ensemble exhibits more style than another tells us nothing in particular about either one. (We shall see later that a similar difficulty arises with the notion of beauty.)

Here, then, is our problem: Is there any way of placing constraints on judgments of taste (for example, on aesthetic judgments) that protects them from the *de gustibus* principle without at the same time relying on spooky nonexplainers? If not, then the whole area can be nothing more than merely dialectical. In fact, however, I see no reason why criticism, for example, has to be dialectical. It can have, if you like, an outside—something that puts constraints on its judgments. To achieve this, it must be deeply immersed in its primary subject matter (works of literature, art, music, and so forth). Although this may seem an odd way of speaking, critics must be involved in *causal* relationships with their subject matter. They must become causally entangled with their subject matter. Hume presents such a view in his essay "Of the Standard of Taste." This essay is, I think, the finest piece written on the theory of criticism.

Hume begins by acknowledging that there is a strong, almost overwhelming presumption against the possibility of establishing standards of taste. First, any such attempt must deal with the wide diversity of taste that exists in the world. Rather than denying this, Hume maintains that the diversity is even wider than most people acknowledge:

Men of the most confined knowledge are able to remark a difference of taste in the narrow circle of their acquaintance, even where the persons have been educated under the same government, and have early imbibed the same prejudices. But those, who can enlarge their view to contemplate distant nations and remote ages, are still more surprized at the great inconsistence and contrariety. We are apt to call *barbarous* whatever departs widely from our own taste and apprehension: But soon find the epithet of reproach retorted on us.[2]

Beyond this, things may be even worse than they first appear, because much that seems to count as agreement in matters of taste is merely verbal:

There are certain terms in every language, which import blame, and others praise; and all men, who use the same tongue, must agree in their application of them. Every voice is united in applauding elegance, propriety, simplicity, spirit in writing; and in blaming fustian, affectation, coldness, and a false brilliancy: But when critics come to particulars, this seeming unanimity vanishes; and it is found, that they had affixed a very different meaning to their expressions.[3]

The mere fact of diversity of opinion does not, by itself, show that no one opinion is better than any other. This is certainly not an attitude that we adopt with respect to simple statements of fact. If one person claims that Jones is at home and another denies this, then there is a fact of the matter that determines which one is right and which one is wrong. Furthermore, there may be a perfectly straightforward procedure for settling this matter beyond reasonable doubt—for example, by searching the house. It seems, however, that Hume can appeal to no parallel check in dealing with conflicts in judgments of taste, for he himself was a subjectivist concerning aesthetic values.

> Among a thousand different opinions which different men may entertain of the same subject, there is one, and but one, that is just and true; and the only difficulty is to fix and ascertain it. On the contrary, a thousand different sentiments, excited by the same object, are all right: Because no sentiment represents what is really in the object.[4]

Beauty, according to Hume, "is no quality in things themselves: It exists merely in the mind which contemplates them; and each mind perceives a different beauty." For Hume, all values, including moral values, arise from sentiments that objects or actions produce in us, which we, without realizing it, project back upon the objects or actions. Thus there is never a value inherent in the object that can confirm or disconfirm our ascription of value to it.

Given this combination of the diversity of taste and the subjectivity of values, we seem forced to accept what Hume calls "the principle of the natural equality of tastes." "De gustibus non disputandum est"—there is no disputing matters of taste. I do not know any place where a stronger argument has been presented against the possibility of establishing standards of taste. Hume cannot be accused of underestimating the difficulty of the task he has undertaken.

Having assembled this powerful argument in behalf of what we might call aesthetic Protagoreanism—each of us is the measure of all values—Hume offers a remarkably simple response to it.

> But though this axiom, by passing into a proverb, seems to have attained the sanction of common sense; there is certainly a species of common sense which opposes it, at least serves to modify and restrain it. Whoever would assert an equality of genius and elegance between OGILBY and MILTON, or BUNYAN and ADDISON, would be thought to defend no less an extravagance, than if he had maintained a mole-hill to be as high as TENERIFFE, or a pond as extensive as the ocean.[5]

The point that Hume is making is this: Although, on one side, the kind of considerations he himself has presented seem to force us to acknowledge the principle of the natural equality of tastes, on the other side, in daily life, we confidently make assessments that run totally counter to that principle.

Many human beings have, for example, wide experience of seeing displays in shop windows, and they usually have definite views concerning which are better than others. There is ample room for disagreement, but when tourists visit Italy they are almost always impressed with the style and elegance of the window displays. This is true not only in fashion centers such as Milan but even of shops in small towns. In comparison, store windows in New York look, if not exactly frumpy, certainly less sophisticated. I have never met anyone—though there may be such—who disagrees with this judgment. But suppose we bring someone who has spent her entire life in a New Guinea village cut off totally from the rest of the world. She has never seen a store window, perhaps not even a store. The objects in the window—the mannequins, various body parts—may strike her as frightening, lewd, dead, ludicrous, and so on, depending on the associations, if any, that she makes. It would not be surprising if her preferences concerning which window looks the most beautiful (or the least ugly) would be strongly at variance with ours. But wouldn't placing our standards above hers simply be a matter of cultural imperialism? If we grant that it is, haven't we undercut the possibility of there being nonarbitrary standards of taste? We seem to be confronted with a dilemma. When we view things up close, as it were, we feel no hesitation in saying that the display in one window is more elegant (imaginative, sophisticated, charming, witty, kicky) than that in another. When, however, we step back and view the situation from a distance—through reflecting on Hume's theoretical criticisms or, more concretely, through reflecting on how the situation might strike others with a different cultural heritage—the confidence in our up close evaluations may simply disappear. Feeling the tug both ways, we are inclined to say something of the following sort: "The food displays in Bologna are absolutely gorgeous—but, of course, there really are no aesthetic values."

Hume's way out of this difficulty (or his way around it) is to treat judgments of taste, at least in their simplest forms, as natural responses to the world. I see (or seem to see) the beauty of a butterfly in the same direct way that I see (or seem to see) the colored pattern of its wings. In fact, it can seem quite impossible to pry the two apart. Wittgenstein notes this in the following passage:

> I know what *this means:* "Imagine this table black instead of brown"; it means something like: "paint a picture of this table, but black instead of brown"; or similarly: "draw this man but with longer legs than he has."
>
> Suppose someone were to say: "Imagine this butterfly exactly as it is, but ugly instead of beautiful"?![6]

Here we want to say—and quite rightly—that it is the colored patterns on the wings that make them beautiful or even constitute the beauty, so it is not possible to pry them apart. Then, however, it could be pointed out that many things are beautiful—for example, pieces of music, which are not composed of colored patterns at all. It seems, then, that the beauty is neither separable from nor locked into the pattern of colors on the butterfly's wings. We seem to be sidetracked by paradox again. Before going further, we will try to find a way of extracting ourselves from it.

Our difficulty here is that we fail to understand the how the word "beautiful"— and, indeed, how evaluative terms in general—function. Hume is on the right track when he remarks, in a passage cited above, that "there are certain terms in every language, which import blame, and others praise." There are, that is, words in our language that express approval or disapproval, or as Hume often puts it, approbation or disapprobation. Evaluative terms such as "good and "beautiful" function to express approval. Words such as "bad" and "ugly" function in the opposite way, to express disapproval. We have an extraordinarily rich and nuanced vocabulary of evaluative terms that allow us to express our approval or disapproval of things in subtle and complex ways. In this vocabulary we find such words as "delicious," "inane," "pompous," "haunting," "elegant," "dainty," and "dumpy." Each of these words provides a way of expressing approval or disapproval (approbation or disapprobation) along a certain axis of evaluation. "Good" is a wholly general term of approbation. It depends entirely on context to have particular force. The word "delicious" has a narrower range of application. It is not the name of a particular flavor; instead, it is our most general term of approbation with respect to flavors.[7]

Our difficulties arise because we tend to think that the notion of beauty is the fundamental notion of aesthetics. If we look at matters this way, we may then think that it is the fundamental task of aesthetics to grasp the essence of this notion. But like the word "good," the word "beautiful," when deprived of contextual support, is nearly contentless. Its use without contextual support amounts to little more than an inane expression of approval along an aesthetic axis. Wittgenstein makes the point in *Culture and Value*. He imagines someone discussing a specific section of a piece of music, saying, "The repeat is necessary." He then offers these reflections on the significance of a remark of this kind:

In what respect is it necessary? Well, sing it, and you
will see that only the repeat gives it its tremendous
power. — Don't we have an impression that a model
for this theme already exists in reality and the theme
only approaches it, corresponds to it, if this section is
repeated? Or am I to utter the inanity: "It just sounds
more beautiful with the repeat"? (There you can see by
the way what an idiotic role the word "beautiful" plays
in aesthetics.) Yet there just *is* no paradigm apart from
the theme itself. And yet again there *is* a paradigm apart
from the theme: namely, the rhythm of our language,
of our thinking and feeling. And the theme, moreover,
is a *new* part of our language; it becomes incorporated
into it; we learn a new *gesture*.[8]

This is rather complex, so perhaps some commentary
is in order. This passage brings out the emptiness or inanity
of saying that a score is better played one way rather than
another because it is more beautiful played that way. The
passage does more than this. It calls our attention to the
feeling that the score, when played in the correct way,
approaches an ideal model that somehow already exists in
reality. When someone says, "Now you have it right," the
word "it" seems to refer to just such an ideal entity that is
being matched. Yet—and this is the central point of this
admittedly difficult passage—there simply is no such pre-
existing model that a performance approximates more or
less closely. There is nothing in back of the theme that
serves as a standard. The theme is not constrained in that
(Platonic) way. Yet the theme does encounter constraints

of a different kind—laterally, we might say. These are "the rhythm of our language, of our thinking and feeling." Though the theme is constrained by the force field that surrounds it, playing the passage in a certain way can make a significant contribution to this field. It provides us, as Wittgenstein puts it, with a new gesture.

We have strayed rather far from Hume's defense of standards of taste. It is time to return. Hume presents what we might call a qualified-spectator account as the basis for such standards.[9] Something will count as a standard of taste if it so recognized by persons of taste. Works of art are then evaluated in terms of these standards. But what qualifies someone to be a person of taste? It will not do to define a person of taste as one who recognizes the appropriate standards. That would be a small circle indeed. Hume attempts to avoid this circle by offering what amounts to a skeptical solution to the skeptical doubts he himself has so forcefully displayed. He offers a description of the conditions under which a reasonable consensus can arise concerning the standards for taste and beauty.

As he did when discussing inductive reasoning, Hume begins by dismissing the idea that the matter at hand can be treated in a purely a priori manner:

> It is evident that none of the rules of composition are fixed by reasonings *a priori,* or can be esteemed abstract conclusions of the understanding, from comparing those habitudes and relations of ideas, which are eternal and immutable. Their foundation is the same with that of all the practical sciences, experience.[10]

If, however, we turn to experience for guidance, we once more encounter the problems of subjectivity and variability. Hume has an ingenious response to this problem. Along with most of his philosophical contemporaries, Hume held that the color of an object is a secondary quality—that is, it is not resident in the object itself but is, instead, something superimposed on it by the mind that perceives it. Hume proposes to treat such qualities as beauty on this model of secondary qualities. This move may seem to give everything away to the skeptic. In the following remarkable passage, which appears as a footnote in his essay "The Sceptic," Hume argues that it does not.

> Were I not afraid of appearing too philosophical, I should remind my reader of that famous doctrine, supposed to be fully proved in modern times, "That tastes and colours, and all other sensible qualities, lie not in the bodies, but merely in the senses." The case is the same with beauty and deformity, virtue and vice. This doctrine, however, takes off no more from the reality of the latter qualities, than from that of the former; nor need it give any umbrage either to critics or moralists. Though colours were allowed to lie only in the eye, would dyers or painters ever be less regarded or esteemed? *There is a sufficient uniformity in the senses and feelings of mankind, to make all these qualities the objects of art and reasoning, and to have the greatest influence on life and manners.* And as it is certain, that the discovery above-mentioned in natural phi-

losophy, makes no alteration on action and conduct;
why should a like discovery in moral philosophy make
any alteration?[11]

That is, we are sufficiently similar in the ways we perceive
and feel about the world to allow a reasonable consensus
to arise concerning qualities of objects of art and reasoning.

There is, however, another source of variability that
must be dealt with: Objects can present different appearances in different settings. Human beings have found ways
for dealing with this problem with respect to colors; Hume
suggests that an analogous method can be used with respect
to beauty.

> If, in the sound state of the organ, there be an entire or
> a considerable uniformity of sentiment among men, we
> may thence derive an idea of the perfect beauty; in like
> manner as the appearance of objects in day-light, to the
> eye of a man in health, is denominated their true and
> real colour, even while colour is allowed to be merely
> a phantasm of the senses.[12]

In "Of the Standard of Taste," Hume develops this
analogy in some detail. Corresponding to the "eye of a man
in health," we have what he calls delicacy of taste:

> Where the organs are so fine, as to allow nothing to
> escape them; and at the same time so exact as to perceive
> every ingredient in the composition: This we call
> delicacy of taste.[13]

It is also necessary, through practice, to develop skills of discernment:

> When objects of any kind are first presented to the eye or imagination, the sentiment, which attends them, is obscure and confused; and the mind is, in a great measure, incapable of pronouncing concerning their merits or defects.[14]

To which Hume adds:

> In a word, the same address and dexterity, which practice gives to the execution of any work, is also acquired by the same means, in the judging of it.[15]

It is also important in developing a sense of taste to see a work of art in its relationship to other works of art:

> A man, who has had no opportunity of comparing the different kinds of beauty, is indeed totally unqualified to pronounce an opinion with regard to any object presented to him. By comparison alone we fix the epithets of praise or blame, and learn how to assign the due degree of each.[16]

It is this lack of comparative experience, not some aesthetic deficiency, that makes the visitor from New Guinea unqualified to judge shop windows.

Finally, as far as possible, a person of taste must be free of bias:

We may observe, that every work of art, in order to produce its due effect on the mind, must be surveyed in a certain point of view, and cannot be fully relished by persons, whose situation, real or imaginary, is not conformable to that which is required by the performance.[17]

In summary:

Strong sense, united to delicate sentiment, improved by practice, perfected by comparison, and cleared of all prejudice, can alone entitle critics to this valuable character; and the joint verdict of such, wherever they are to be found, is the true standard of taste and beauty.[18]

For Hume, then, proper aesthetic appreciation involves a complex interaction between feeling and thought. In his *Enquiry Concerning the Principles of Morals* he makes the point this way:

Some species of beauty, especially the natural kinds, on their first appearance, command our affection and approbation; and where they fail of this effect, it is impossible for any reasoning to redress their influence, or adapt them better to our taste and sentiment. But in many orders of beauty, particularly those of the finer arts, it is requisite to employ much reasoning, in order to feel the proper sentiment; and a false relish may frequently be corrected by argument and reflection.[19]

I have only two reservations about Hume's account of standards of taste. The first concerns Hume's tendency to pitch the discussion at too a high a level by concentrating on beauty, even on perfect beauty. The second reservation concerns Hume's claim that the principles of taste are universal, which suggests that all persons of taste, wherever and whenever they have lived, will arrive at the same fundamental principles of taste. Though there is no a priori reason why this could not be true, I do not see any reason for supposing (or demanding) that standards of taste will—in some deep-down manner—be invariant over different cultures, times, and subject matters. Persons meeting Hume's qualifications for being arbiters of taste can exert their talents in cultures having forms of art and artistic traditions unlike those found in Hume's (or our) culture. Nothing in Hume's argument forces a commitment to universality. Skepticism does not automatically win if the universality of the standards of taste is not established. Hume's basic argument is not directed against pluralism with respect to standards of taste; it is directed against what he calls "the principle of the natural equality of tastes." The distinction between persons with taste and those lacking it remains, even if the distinction manifests itself in different ways in different cultures and perhaps even in different ways in different aspects of a particular culture.[20]

In closing, let me return to the comparison between Hume's skeptical solution to his philosophical doubts concerning induction and his skeptical solution to his philosophical doubts concerning standards of taste. In both cases Hume's solution is essentially causal. It is our interaction with the world around us that allows us (with luck) to form stable and reasonably accurate beliefs about the laws governing nature. Similarly, it is our interactions with art, music, and literature that allow us to make stable and reasonably accurate judgments concerning the standards governing taste. In each case, when we immerse ourselves in something nonconceptual, constraints are put on our judgments. If, on the contrary, we look in the opposite direction, to theory, to solve our problems, we will, I believe, inevitably be driven into one of two opposing positions, an a priori view concerning ideal entities or a perspectivist/skeptical view that denigrates objects of art. Either way, criticism loses contact with its subject matter.

The evaporation of subject matter is the central threat to significant work in the humanities and, for that matter, in the social sciences as well. The recent addiction to what is called "critical theory" is a central force in this drive toward emptiness.

To learn is to learn to have fun.

W.V.O. Quine, *The Roots of Reference*

CHAPTER SEVEN

Last Words

An examination of the precarious character of our intellectual lives has the following disturbing feature: Reflecting on the ways in which our intellectual lives can come to be precarious can yield the belief that they really are hopelessly precarious. I have argued, for example, that by placing no restrictions on the defeators we take seriously in evaluating knowledge claims, we are led straight into skepticism. Paradoxically, reflecting on remote defeators and the harm that arises from taking them seriously can lead us to take them seriously and thus put ourselves in harm's way.[1]

One way out of this difficulty is to hold that skeptical problems, though intellectually puzzling, can never be taken seriously. This, as Hume saw, is simply false. Having raised a series of skeptical challenges that he finds wholly unanswerable, Hume attempts to find solace in the thought that "very refin'd reflections have little or no influence on us." He sees at once that this will not do:

> But what have I here said, that reflections very refin'd and metaphysical have little or no influence upon us? This opinion I can scarce forbear retracting, and condemning from my present feeling and experience. The *intense* view of these manifold contradictions and imperfections in human reason has so wrought upon me, and heated my brain, that I am ready to reject all belief and reasoning, and can look upon no opinion even as more probable or likely than another. Where am I, or what? From what causes do I derive my existence, and to what condition shall I return? Whose favour shall I court, and whose anger must I dread? What beings surround me? and on whom have I any influence, or who have any influence on me? I am confounded with all these questions, and begin to fancy myself in the most deplorable condition imaginable, inviron'd with the deepest darkness, and utterly depriv'd of the use of every member and faculty.[2]

When doing philosophy one can become seriously spooked.

It seems, then, that examining the precarious life of a rational animal is itself an inherently precarious activity. So why engage in it? Hume addresses this question in both the *Treatise of Human Nature* and in the *Enquiry Concerning Human Understanding*. The answer in the *Treatise* comes to this: Although doing philosophy can yield melancholy, sometimes—when the situation is right—it can also be fun. In Hume's more dignified language:

> At the time, therefore, that I am tir'd with amusement and company, and have indulg'd a *reverie* in my chamber, or in a solitary walk by a river-side, I feel my mind all collected within itself, and am naturally *inclin'd* to carry my view into all those subjects, about which I have met with so many disputes in the course of my reading and conversation. I cannot forbear having a curiosity to be acquainted with the principles of moral good and evil, the nature and foundation of government, and the cause of those several passions and inclinations, which actuate and govern me. . . . These sentiments spring up naturally in my present disposition; and shou'd I endeavour to banish them, by attaching myself to any other business or diversion, I *feel* I shou'd be a loser in point of pleasure; and this is the origin of my philosophy.[3]

I am in complete sympathy with this justification for engaging in philosophy, but in his *Enquiry Concerning Human Understanding* Hume takes the matter deeper. In the opening section of this work he draws a distinction between two kinds of philosophy, one popular (or easy), the other abstruse.

> [Popular or easy philosophy] considers man chiefly as
>> born for action; and as influenced in his measures
>> by taste and sentiment. . . .
> [Abstruse philosophers] consider man in the light of a
>> reasonable rather than an active being, and endeav-
>> our to form his understanding more than cultivate
>> his manners.[4]

Hume points out various disadvantages in engaging in abstruse philosophy. It can have little influence on daily life. It is easy to go wrong when pursuing it. Echoing the passage from the *Treatise* cited above, he also points out that doing abstruse philosophy can make one feel quite miserable. He has Nature herself issue the following warning to those who would engage in abstruse philosophy:

> Abstruse thought and profound researches I prohibit, and
> will severely punish, by the pensive melancholy which
> they introduce, by the endless uncertainty in which they
> involve you, and by the cold reception which your
> pretended discoveries shall meet with, when communi-
> cated. Be a philosopher; but, amidst all your philosophy,
> be still a man.[5]

Given all this, why should any sensible person pursue abstruse philosophy? Hume owes his reader an answer to this question, for the remainder of the *Enquiry Concerning Human Understanding* is itself a specimen of abstruse philosophy.

Hume offers a number of responses to this challenge. He tells us that the study of abstruse philosophy can contribute to accurate thinking—perhaps in the way that the study of geometry is said to do this. Repeating the claim that he made in the *Treatise,* he tells us that sometimes, for some people, engaging in abstruse reflections can be pleasurable. He then offers a much deeper reason for undertaking the labors of abstruse philosophy:

> The only method of freeing learning, at once, from these abstruse questions, is to enquire seriously into the nature of human understanding, and show, from an exact analysis of its powers and capacity, that it is by no means fitted for such remote and abstruse subjects. We must submit to this fatigue, in order to live at ease ever after.[6]

The fundamental reason for pursuing abstruse philosophy is, in the end, to free ourselves of the need and desire to do so.

It is only in the final section of the *Enquiry Concerning Human Understanding* that Hume indicates how this catharsis can take place. Although Hume holds that skeptical doubts lose much of their force when philosophers leave their studies and return to the affairs of daily life, he does not hold that skeptical doubts are wholly devoid of influence on daily life. For Hume, doubts raised in the study can, though with diminished force, be carried out to the streets, where they can perform the useful service of moderating dogmatic commitments. In this way, skeptical doubts can be used to curb what Hume refers to as "enthusiasm"—what we now call fanaticism.

For Hume, recognition of the force of skeptical arguments can have another salutary effect: It can place limits on the scope of our intellectual activities. In a passage that in some ways anticipates Kant's notion of dialectical illusions, Hume tells us:

> The *imagination* of man is naturally sublime, delighted with whatever is remote and extraordinary, and running, without control, into the most distant parts of space and time in order to avoid the objects, which custom has rendered too familiar to it. A correct *Judgment* observes a contrary method, and avoiding all distant and high enquiries, confines itself to common life, and to such subjects as fall under daily practice and experience; leaving the more sublime topics to the embellishment of poets and orators, or to the arts of priests and politicians. To bring us to so salutary a determination, nothing can be more serviceable, than to be once thoroughly convinced of the force of the Pyrrhonian doubt, and of the impossibility, that any thing, but the strong power of natural instinct, could free us from it.[7]

For Hume, then, contexts in which radically skeptical doubts emerge and contexts in which our beliefs are generated by natural instincts are not discrete, isolated domains. Each influences the other. Without the powerful force of natural belief, nothing can stop reason's inevitable slide into forlorn skepticism. Without the humbling force of skeptical doubts, nothing prevents our thoughts from going beyond their natural limits into the land of illusions. It is only through the pursuit of abstruse philosophy that we can gain a proper understanding of our cognitive limitations, an understanding that will allow us, in Hume's words, "to live at ease ever after."

My own views are broadly in agreement with Hume's—not surprisingly, because his writings are where many of them come from. There are, however, some differences. In chapter 5, I argued that Hume was overly pessimistic in describing the limits of science, for many of the things that he thought would forever lie beyond our understanding (for example, why bread nourishes) are now well understood. Unlike Hume, I see no limits in principle to how far science can progress. On the other side, it seems to me that Hume, at least in the passages just cited, was overly optimistic in thinking that we can reach a stable point in our intellectual lives where we can "live at ease ever after." With Kant and Wittgenstein, I think that precariousness is a permanent feature of our intellectual lives. If that is right, then philosophers have an important role to play in exposing the mechanisms that persistently distort and corrupt our intellectual activities. If this is a humble activity, at least it is one that will always be needed.

Isn't all this a bit of a downer? In a way it is. If Kant is right in saying, "Human reason . . . is burdened by questions which . . . it is not able to ignore, but which, as transcending all its powers, it is also not able to answer," then we are doomed to either illusion or dissatisfaction. Agreeing with Kant, I find this result inescapable. But it is not a result that closes off all inquiry or makes all inquiry dull. I have suggested that the only thing—or at least the chief thing— that protects us from falling into incoherence, from being captured by dialectical illusion, and from succumbing to an abject skepticism is becoming engaged in the world in ways that put our thoughts under constraints that are not themselves further thoughts. This is an inherently fallible, risky, and often disappointing activity. It is not, however, an inherently dull activity. It is often fun and, at its best, high adventure.

NOTES

INTRODUCTION

1. This is Einstein's revision of his earlier, more famous, and more dignified remark, "God is subtle, but he is not malicious."

2. Unless otherwise indicated, references to God will be to a standard-issue deity of a Judeo-Christian-Islamic sort.

3. This is in some ways similar to William James's notion that an option is "genuine" when it is "forced, living, and momentous." An option is forced, James tells us, if it is "based on a complete logical disjunction, with no possibility of not choosing." Whether an option is forced or not depends on how the option is formulated. For example, accepting God's existence or not accepting God's existence is a forced option. On the other hand, the choice between theism and atheism is not forced because there is a third alternative, agnosticism. It is, I believe, more interesting to reflect on how options (forced or not) can become living and momentous. This is the kind of inquiry I pursue here. For James's views on these matters, see his *Will to Believe,* 3ff.

4. Sartre, *Existentialism,* 26–27. It should be noted that Sartre later abandoned many of the ideas expressed in this passage, but this does not make it any less arresting.

5. Lewis, *Analysis of Knowledge and Valuation,* 186. Annette Baier called this passage to my attention.

6. I do consider them in extended detail in part 2 of *Pyrrhonian Reflections.*

7. Lewis, *Analysis of Knowledge and Valuation,* 186.

8. Hume presents just such an argument in his *Treatise,* 121–25.

9. Wittgenstein, *Philosophical Investigations,* #111.
10. Kant, *Critique of Pure Reason,* 7.
11. Kant, *Prolegomena,* 99.
12. Hume, *Treatise,* 218.

CHAPTER ONE

1. Aristotle, in his effort to understand the laws of logic, almost single-handedly, it seems, brought the science of logic into existence—a truly stunning intellectual achievement.

2. The traditional Big Three fundamental laws of logic are completed by two others: the law of identity (everything is identical with itself) and the law of excluded middle (something is either the case or not the case). Except for some asides, I will not consider these laws but concentrate on the law of non-contradiction.

3. Aristotle, *Metaphysics,* in *Complete Works,* 4.3.1005b19–20.

4. Ibid., 4.3.1005a24–25.

5. The notion that a false or even nonsensical philosophical conception can force itself on us through our tendency to adopt a faulty picture of how our language functions is one of Ludwig Wittgenstein's leading ideas. Reflecting on mistakes found in his own earlier writings, he remarks:

> A *picture* held us captive. And we could not get outside it,
> for it lay in our language and language seemed to repeat it
> to us inexorably. (*Philosophical Investigations,* #115)

In this chapter I am trying to describe, or at least sketch, the picture that leads people to misunderstand the status of the law of noncontradiction.

6. Heracleitus of Ephesus, an early pre-Socratic (c. 500 B.C.), is famous for employing the metaphor that the world is composed of fire.

7. Some classical scholars deny that Heracleitus rejected the law of noncontradiction. But Aristotle thought that he did, as did other ancient commentators. In any case, even if Heracleitus

will not serve our symbolic purposes, his follower Cratylus, who outdid his master by saying that one cannot step in the same river even once, will. According to Aristotle, Cratylus was so deeply committed to the doctrine of endless change or universal flux that he thought it impossible to assert anything at all, holding that the meanings of the words at the beginning of a sentence would change before the sentence was completed. Cratylus, again according to Aristotle, was thus reduced to pointing his finger at things as they passed. (See *Metaphysics,* in *Complete Works,* 4.5.1009a7–16.)

8. For example, Nietzsche praises Heracleitus in "Twilight of the Idols," in *Portable Nietzsche,* 480.

9. Parmenides of Elea (c. 480 B.C.), like Heracleitus, was an early pre-Socratic. Little survives of his writings, but traditionally he has been associated with the view that the world, in its really real aspects, is one, perfect and unchanging. His student Zeno (c. 470 B.C.) famously produced a series of paradoxes intended to show the impossibility of change or motion.

10. As in "Goodbye, Ruby Tuesday, / Who could hang a name on you? / When you change with every new day. . . ."

11. The most extreme change in the course of nature would be for it to go completely out of existence—a possibility entertained by theologians and, I have been told, by contemporary cosmologists.

12. Hegel, *Phenomenology of Mind,* 105.

13. Wittgenstein, *Notebooks, 1914–1916,* 37. By logical constants, Wittgenstein had in mind such logical expressions as "and," "or," "if . . . , then . . . ," "all," "some," and so on.

14. Wittgenstein, *Tractatus,* proposition 4.0312: "My fundamental idea is that the 'logical constants' are not representatives; that there can be no representatives of the *logic* of facts."

15. There is something right about this claim that meaningful symbols are more than marks on paper or vibrations in air. What is wrong is the assumption that all words get their meanings essentially in the same way that names do—by referring to or standing for things.

16. Some may think that, in equating the meaning of an expression with the job it performs, I am attributing a view to Wittgenstein's early writings that is found only in his later writings. This is wrong. Wittgenstein's initial break with a purely referential conception of language occurs first in the *Tractatus* with respect to logical terms and numbers. In his later writings, Wittgenstein expands this attack on the referential conception of language, with the result that much of the *Tractatus* itself is rejected root and branch. I discuss these matters in *Wittgenstein* and "Wittgenstein's Critique of Philosophy."

17. Unfortunately, when writers of logic texts introduce truth-table definitions, they rarely comment on their deep philosophical significance.

18. Quine, *From Stimulus to Science,* 23.

19. Aristotle, *Metaphysics,* in *Complete Works,* 4.3.1006a5–11.

20. Ibid., 4.4.1006a12–28.

21. The standard proof that everything follows from a contradiction depends on three seemingly unassailable principles. The first concerns conjunction. From the conjunction $p \mathrel{\&} q$ we may infer p and we may also infer q. The second concerns disjunction: from p, we may infer p or q. The third principle also concerns disjunction and is a bit more complicated: from p or q, together with $\sim p$, we may infer q. Given these three rules of inference, the proof of the spread principle—the principle that everything follows from a contradiction—is short and sweet:

$p \mathrel{\&} \sim p$	
p	The conjunction principle
$p \lor q$	The first disjunction principle
$\sim p$	The conjunction principle again
q	The second disjunction principle

Because q can be any proposition whatsoever, this proof shows that if we start with a contradiction, we can derive any proposition we please. In order to block this line of reasoning, at least one of the three inference rules that generate it must be rejected. This makes tough intuitive going, because each of these three inference rules seems wholly plausible on its face. Even so, attempts have been made to construct logical systems that block this argument. I will not go into this here.

22. Not only will the contrast between asserting and denying be undercut, but a whole range of other speech acts will be compromised as well—for example, promising to do something as opposed to promising not to, asking someone to do something as opposed to asking that person not to, and so on through a wide range of different types of speech acts.

23. I recently found a variation on Aristotle's negative demonstration of the laws of logic in Daniel Dennett's *Darwin's Dangerous Idea*. Confronted with a theologian who holds that "faith is quite beyond reason," Dennett suggests the following rejoinder:

> The philosopher Ronald de Sousa once memorably described philosophical theology as "intellectual tennis without a net," and I readily allow that I have indeed been assuming without comment or question . . . that the net of rational judgment was up. But we can lower it if you really want to. It's your serve. Whatever you serve, suppose I return service rudely as follows: "What you say implies that God is a ham sandwich wrapped in tinfoil. That's not much of a God to worship!" If you then volley back, demanding to know how I can logically justify my claim that your serve has such a preposterous implication, I will reply: "Oh, do you want the net up for my returns, but not for your serves? Either the net stays up, or it stays down. If the net is down, there are no rules and anybody can say anything, a mug's game if there ever was one. I have been giving you the benefit of the assumption that you would not waste your own time or mine by playing with the net down." (154)

This doesn't refute the theologian's claim, for various responses are open to him. There is the Zen move: "Is God a ham sandwich wrapped in tinfoil? Yes. We can say that too."

And our fideistic theologian may take absolute delight in the thought that we have to play with the net up, whereas he doesn't. Such theologians and many so-called postmodern thinkers exist quite beyond the reach of intellectual embarrassment, except, that is, when their position carries with it *personal* disadvantages. It is for this reason that I prefer the cruder version of an ad hominem attack of the kind given above.

24. Seeing that the law of noncontradiction is equally compatible with the possibility and the impossibility of change clears away one obstacle to understanding change. However, that by itself does not make change an unproblematic notion. Zeno's paradoxes remain a challenge to the *intelligibility,* if not the possibility, of change.

CHAPTER TWO

1. This example was a favorite of Wilfrid Sellars.
2. This is no more than a crude first approximation of a complex matter. Our language is governed by a wide variety of rules that function in many different ways. All this needs sorting out, but that is not possible here.
3. Wittgenstein, *Philosophical Investigations,* #43.
4. As I read Wittgenstein, the identification of meaning with use appears in a limited way in his early work *Tractatus Logico-Philosophicus.* As his commitment to the "meaning equals use" doctrine expanded in later years, Wittgenstein came to reject large and central portions of this earlier work. The opening hundred or so sections of his *Philosophical Investigations* tell this story. I have spelled it out in detail in my book *Wittgenstein.* Not everyone reads Wittgenstein on this as I do.
5. It is actually a blend of two of Wittgenstein's examples from his *Remarks on the Foundations of Mathematics*, part 3, #77, and part 7, #29. I tried these ideas out first in a paper presented at a conference in Bristol, England, in 1974, later published as "Hintikka's Game Theoretic Approach to Language" in 1976.

6. The rule in checkers is actually more complicated, but that does not matter here.

7. The conflict in rules can take other forms; for example, a move may be both permitted and forbidden.

8. I defended this interpretation of Wittgenstein's treatment of inconsistency in "Wittgenstein's Critique of Philosophy."

9. It seems natural to attribute the use of language to other animals as well: pets, honeybees, and trained apes, for example. It is probably idle to ask whether these animals *really* possess a language. It is enough to note that some animals sometimes exhibit behavior that is strikingly similar to human linguistic behavior. In such cases it may be useful to describe and attempt to explain animal behavior using linguistic categories. Just how useful this will be remains to be seen. So far, under even the most generous interpretation of the data, no animal has ever been shown to command more than a small fragment of the linguistic capacities of humans. It may be an error to say that the command of language is a distinctive feature of human beings, but (ignoring spirits) it comes very close to being one of our distinctive features.

10. Eubulides of Miletus is thought to have been a contemporary of Aristotle. Beyond his being a compiler of paradoxes, little more is known about him.

11. A popular discussion of this theorem is found in Hoftstader, *Gödel, Escher, Bach*.

12. Tarski, "The Concept of Truth in Formalized Languages," 164–65.

13. Wittgenstein, *Zettel,* #691.

14. Wittgenstein, *Remarks on the Foundations of Mathematics,* part 4, #56.

15. It is possible that a situation could arise in which the liar paradox interfered with serious practical activity. Perhaps a computer program incorporating some variant of a liar sentence would constantly crash or go into an infinite loop. The obvious counsel would be to look for a way of writing the program that did not incorporate liar sentences—just as in

writing programs one must avoid instructions that involve division by zero. It could turn out, however, that self-referential sentences akin to liar sentences are needed in order to achieve the programmer's aims. The task then would be to find some way of employing such expressions without generating crashes or infinite loops. In that case, something would have to be done about the paradox, but what exactly was done would be closely tied to the specific task that the program was supposed to perform. It need not involve finding a solution to the liar paradox in general. In a practical context, a practical solution would be good enough—perhaps an intellectual triumph.

16. For a detailed defense of the existence of moral dilemmas, see Marcus, "Moral Dilemmas and Consistency," and Sinnott-Armstrong, *Moral Dilemmas*.

17. James, "The Moral Philosopher and the Moral Life," in *Will to Believe,* 188.

18. Perhaps such deontological instincts have been hardwired into us by evolutionary forces. If true, this would explain their strong and almost universal appeal. It would not, however, establish their moral legitimacy. A consequentialist could acknowledge that, for the most part, deontological instincts promote the common good and for this reason they should, for the most part, be followed. Yet when they yield results that are deeply contrary to the common good, they should be set aside. The unwillingness to do so even in extreme cases could be treated as a genetic defect.

19. William James expressed a similar belief when he wrote, "There is really no more ground for supposing that all our [moral] demands can be accounted for by one universal underlying kind of motive than there is ground for supposing that all physical phenomena are cases of a single law. The elementary forces in ethics are probably as plural as those in physics are" ("The Moral Philosopher and the Moral Life," in *Will to Believe,* 201). Of course, if the dream of a unified field theory is fulfilled, then James will have turned out to be wrong about physics. Perhaps he (and I) may prove to be mistaken

about ethics. So far, at least, the prospects do not look good for a unified field theory in ethics.

20. Ruth Barcan Marcus makes this point in "Moral Dilemmas and Consistency."

21. Conflicts can arise in a consequentialist theory if it admits a plurality of goods with no systematic way of ranking them.

22. Sartre, *Existentialism,* 28–32.

23. This diagram originally came from Jastrow, *Fact and Fable in Psychology.*

24. It is a commonplace that those engaged in litigation often become passionately committed to the rectitude of positions that in the eyes of others are altogether hopeless.

25. As the practices of "sharp" lawyers have shown, any legal situation can be destabilized, given enough resources to pursue unrestricted zealous advocacy. Our legal system often buckles under such pounding. It continues to function in large measure because most litigants and defendants do not have the resources (or perhaps the stomach) to bring such pressure to bear against it.

CHAPTER THREE

1. See Kant, *Critique of Pure Reason,* A51.

2. Quine, *Word and Object,* 2.

3. More precisely: "The understanding does not derive its laws (a priori) from, but prescribes them to, nature." Kant, *Prolegomena,* section 36.

4. Noam Chomsky's notion that all natural languages, despite their surface differences, are based upon a shared system of linguistic universals provides another example of a framework that is shared by all (sane) human beings. On his approach, we can again understand how it is possible for one person to understand another. We can also understand how it is possible to give reasonably good translations from one language to another even when the surface grammar of the two languages is strikingly dissimilar. For more on this, seem Noam

Chomsky's classic *Cartesian Linguistics* and Stephen Pinker's accessible book *The Language Instinct.*

5. Some scholars have held that the Protagorean dictum that man is the measure of all things refers to humankind in general, not to people individually, thus making Protagoras a species chauvinist. Plato, who was closer to Protagoras than we are, did not understand him this way, nor shall I.

6. Alexander Nehamas gives a sympathetic account of Nietzsche's perspectivism in *Nietzsche: Life as Literature.*

7. Though it is not altogether easy to give a precise statement of the Whorf hypothesis, it has had a wide (and to my mind largely unfortunate) influence. For his side of the story, see Whorf, *Language, Thought, and Reality.*

8. Donald Davidson's "On the Very Idea of a Conceptual Scheme" offers a well-known critique of the notion that competing conceptual schemes can wall people off from one another. It is reprinted in his *Inquiries into Truth and Interpretation.*

9. John Searle presents a detailed and accessible theory of social constructs, including sharp criticisms of those who base extreme relativistic conclusions on this notion, in his *Construction of Social Reality.*

10. Plato, *Theaetetus* 171a–b, 298.

11. A similar sense of profundity can attach itself to the sentence "Everything is connected," where it doesn't seem to matter what the connections actually are. One is simply impressed with the togetherness of things.

12. I owe this insight to a joke told to me by Harry Frankfurt.

13. This theme runs throughout Dewey's writings, assuming the title role in his *Quest for Certainty.*

14. Hume, *History of England,* 6:574.

15. Kant, *Critique of Pure Reason*, 99.

16. Kant thought the various forms that dialectical illusions can take are grounded in the various forms that arguments take. Few find this aspect of his position persuasive. Because this doctrine is not necessary for my purposes, I will not go into it.

17. Wittgenstein expressed a similar view in these words:

> One thinks that one is tracing the outline of the thing's nature over and over again, and one is merely tracing round the frame through which we look at it. (*Philosophical Investigations*, #114)

18. Kant did, however, hold that certain ethical considerations can provide a rational basis for positing the existence of God, along with the freedom of the will, and the immortality of the soul. I wish he hadn't.

19. Hume, *Dialogues Concerning Natural Religion,* 161.

20. Ibid., 163.

21. Ibid.

22. Someone else has made this point, but I cannot now remember who it was.

23. Kant, *Critique of Pure Reason,* 47.

CHAPTER FOUR

1. Clifford, "Ethics of Belief," 186.

2. Such an alliance between skepticism and faith has a long history. It is reflected in Martin Luther's remark that reason is a blind whore, at least with respect to the fundamental mysteries of the Christian religion. An even stronger version of this view is possible: Being repugnant to reason can make something all the more worthy of being an object of faith. This view is captured in the motto "Credo quia absurdum est" ("I believe because it is absurd"), attributed to the second- and third-century theologian Tertullian, though perhaps, as some commentators think, not accurately.

3. Descartes, *Philosophical Writings,* 2:15. The continuation of this passage is interesting in showing Descartes's understanding of the contextualist character of belief.

> But this is an arduous undertaking, and a kind of laziness brings me back to normal life. I am like a prisoner who is enjoying an imaginary freedom while asleep; as he begins

> to suspect that he is asleep, he dreads being woken up, and
> goes along with the pleasant illusion as long as he can. In
> the same way, I happily slide back into my old opinions
> and dread being shaken out of them, for fear that my
> peaceful sleep may be followed by hard labour when I
> wake, and that I shall have to toil not in the light, but amid
> the inextricable darkness of the problems I have now
> raised.

This de facto report of the difficulty in maintaining philosophical concentration is similar to remarks found in David Hume's writings. There is a difference, however. For Hume, as we shall see, this incapacity provides our sole defense against radical doubt.

4. Fogelin, *Pyrrhonian Reflections,* especially chapters 1 and 5.
5. Wittgenstein, *On Certainty,* #344.
6. Wittgenstein, *Tractatus,* 6.51.
7. Concerning the intelligibility of skepticism, I agree with Michael Williams, who tells us:

> The fact is that we seem to understand the sceptic very
> well, and certainly well enough to understand how to
> argue against him or why so many popular antisceptical
> arguments fail. It is therefore difficult for us to convince
> ourselves that we do not understand the sceptic at all.
> (*Unnatural Doubts*, xiv)

Although Williams and I are in agreement concerning the intelligibility of skepticism, we are on opposite sides of the question whether skeptical challenges can be met. He thinks that they all can be met; I think that many of them cannot.

8. Though there has been some controversy on the matter, it is generally thought that Hume himself was the author of the *Abstract.* For the present purposes, it does not matter who the author was, because whoever wrote it gave Hume's skeptical argument concerning induction its most elegant statement.
9. Hume, *Abstract,* 651–52.

10. Kant, in his attempt to answer Hume's skepticism concerning induction, maintained that the mind structures experience in a way that guarantees that experience obeys the principle of the uniformity of nature. Thus the claim that nature is uniform is, for him, an a priori truth. In response, two things are worth noting. First, nothing like a consensus exists that Kant actually established this claim. Second, even if it is an a priori truth that nature must be uniform, Hume could restate his argument in a way that would preserve its skeptical force. Suppose we grant, following Kant, that if the sun does or does not rise tomorrow, there must be a determinate cause for whichever event actually occurs. Still, it remains an empirical question just what that cause is. So no matter how much empirical evidence we have, it will always remain the case that further evidence will show that we have *misidentified* the true cause. Nothing in Kant's position, even assuming that it is correct, rules out this possibility, so the skeptical threat remains unanswered.

11. Quine, "Epistemology Naturalized," 72.

12. Descartes, *Philosophical Writings,* 1:122.

13. Translations of Sextus's writings can be found in *Sextus Empiricus.*

14. This account of Pyrrhonian skepticism, especially the concluding remarks, has been the subject of a sharp controversy in the recent literature on Pyrrhonism. Borrowing the distinction from Galen, Jonathan Barnes contrasts two ways of interpreting late Pyrrhonism: as either a *rustic* or an *urbane* skepticism. Treated as a rustic, the Pyrrhonist is pictured as setting aside subtlety and flat-footedly seeking suspension of belief on all matters whatsoever, including the practical beliefs concerning everyday life. In contrast to this rustic interpretation, the view that I adopt follows the urbane interpretation defended in detail by Michael Frede. On this reading, the targets of Pyrrhonian skepticism are dogmatic philosophers and their fellow travelers. The Pyrrhonists' aim is not a universal suspension of belief, but instead a suspension of belief on philosophical (and related) matters. With respect to ordinary beliefs, the Pyrrhonian

skeptic thinks, speaks, and believes as others do. These matters are discussed in the introduction to Fogelin, *Pyrrhonian Reflections*. For Frede's detailed discussion of this topic, see his "Skeptic's Beliefs."

15. See Sextus Empiricus, *Outlines of Pyrrhonism,* in book 1, 114–17, and book 2, chapters 2–7, in *Sextus Empiricus*, vol. 1.

16. Ibid., book 1, 164.

17. See ibid., book 1, chapter 14.

18. Because of their complete generality, they may also seem to show that Jonathan Barnes and others are correct in treating Pyrrhonists as rustic skeptics.

19. Sextus Empiricus, *Against the Logicians,* book 2, 481, in *Sextus Empiricus,* vol. 2.

20. Sextus Empiricus, *Outlines of Pyrrhonism,* book 1, 206–7, in *Sextus Empiricus,* vol. 1.

21. BonJour, *Structure of Empirical Knowledge,* 21.

22. Recently there has been an asymptotic (and largely unacknowledged) drift in the direction of Pyrrhonism, but I cannot go into this here. I discuss the matter in "The Skeptics Are Coming! The Skeptics Are Coming!" an article whose publication is still coming.

23. I got this example from Ernest Sosa. In conversation, Sosa said that he got it from Carl Genet. I discuss this example in detail in *Pyrrhonian Reflections,* 25–26.

24. This approach could be modeled on Paul Grice's important essay "Logic and Conversation," reprinted in his *Studies in the Way of Words,* 22–40.

CHAPTER FIVE

1. Hume, *Treatise,* 268–69.

2. Ibid., 269.

3. Hume, *Enquiry Concerning Human Understanding,* 54–55.

4. Wittgenstein, *Philosophical Investigations,* #472–73.

5. Hume, *Enquiry Concerning Human Understanding,* 161–62.

6. Ibid., 32–33 (emphasis added).

7. Ibid., 162.
8. Feyerabend, *Against Method,* 3.
9. Ibid., 19.
10. Ibid., 18.
11. Ibid., 32.
12. Bacon, *Works of Francis Bacon,* vol. 4, *Great Instauration,* 14.
13. Ibid., 95.
14. Feyerabend, *Against Method,* 232.
15. Hume, *Treatise,* 268.

CHAPTER SIX

1. Hume, as we shall see, alludes to this principle, describing it as an axiom that has passed into a proverb. It is unclear, however, where this principle comes from. There seem to be no exact counterparts in ancient texts, and, somewhat surprisingly, the earliest explicit statement of this principle turned up thus far is found in Laurence Sterne's *Tristram Shandy* (1759). There are, however, numerous occurrences of the related maxim concerning the diversity of taste, including Homer's "Different men take joy in different things" (*Odyssey* 14.228), Archilochus's "Some please themselves in one way, others in another" (25 West; 41 Diehl), and Lucretius's "One man's meat is another man's poison" (*On the Nature of Things,* book 4, 638). This ancient wisdom survives in the contemporary saying "Different strokes for different folks." I owe this display of scholarship entirely to Virginia Close and William Moran, both retired members of the superb staff of reference librarians at Dartmouth College's Baker/Berry Library.
2. Hume, "Of the Standard of Taste," in *Essays,* 226–27.
3. Ibid., 227.
4. Ibid., 230.
5. Ibid., 230–31.
6. Wittgenstein, *Philosophical Grammar,* #127.
7. The word "delicious" can be used metaphorically with respect

to other things; for example, we can speak of a delicious satire or (proverbially) of a delicious blonde. There are, however, limits to the ways in which specialized evaluative terms can be used metaphorically. I know what it is like for a shortstop to make a beautiful play, but I can attach no meaning to the idea of a shortstop making a delicious play.

8. Wittgenstein, *Culture and Value*, 52.

9. This is a more modest notion than that of an *ideal* spectator who judges things from a godlike perspective. Hume spells out in detail the features a person must possess in order to be a qualified judge of aesthetic matters.

10. Hume, "Of the Standard of Taste," in *Essays*, 231.

11. Hume, "The Sceptic," in *Essays*, 166 (emphasis added).

12. Hume, "Of the Standard of Taste," in *Essays*, 234.

13. Ibid., 235.

14. Ibid., 237.

15. Ibid.

16. Ibid., 238.

17. Ibid., 239.

18. Ibid., 241.

19. Hume, *Enquiry Concerning Principles of Morals*, 173. The passage continues with the claim that a similar situation holds for moral standards:

> There are just grounds to conclude, that moral beauty partakes much of this latter species, and demands the assistance of our intellectual faculties, in order to give it a suitable influence on the human mind.

This represents an interesting reversal of the common way of reasoning. Usually the claim that moral standards are like aesthetic standards is a way of indicating their complete subjectivity. Here Hume, as a defender of standards of taste, invokes this comparison in support of the possibility of reasonably objective moral standards.

20. Given their capacity for making sound judgments in their own cultural settings, people of taste may have an advantage in

understanding and appreciating the values of other cultures. In doing so, they may also widen the range of comparisons that they take to be aesthetically relevant.

CHAPTER SEVEN

1. This is a central theme of Fogelin, *Pyrrhonian Reflections.* A somewhat different, though parallel, line of thought can be found in David Lewis, "Elusive Knowledge."
2. Hume, *Treatise,* 268–69.
3. Ibid., 270–71.
4. Hume, *Enquiry Concerning Human Understanding*, 5–6.
5. Ibid., 9.
6. Ibid., 12.
7. Ibid., 162.

BIBLIOGRAPHY

Aristotle. *The Complete Works of Aristotle*. Ed. Jonathan Barnes. 2 vols. Princeton: Princeton University Press, 1984.

Austin, J. L. *Philosophical Papers*. Ed. J. O. Urmson and G. J. Warnock. 3rd ed. Oxford: Oxford University Press, 1979.

Bacon, Francis. *The Works of Francis Bacon*. Ed. Robert Ellis, James Spedding, and Douglas Heath. 14 vols. London: Longmans, 1889.

Barnes, Jonathan. "The Beliefs of a Pyrrhonist." In *Proceedings of the Cambridge Philological Society,* ed. E. J. Kenny and M. M. MacKenzie, 1982: 2–29.

BonJour, Laurence. *The Structure of Empirical Knowledge*. Cambridge, Mass.: Harvard University Press, 1985.

Burnyeat, Myles. "Can the Sceptic Live His Scepticism?" In *Doubt and Dogmatism,* ed. M. Schofield, M. F. Burnyeat, and J. Barnes. Oxford: Clarendon Press, 1980.

Chomsky, Noam. *Cartesian Linguistics*. New York: Harper and Row, 1966.

Clifford, W. K. "The Ethics of Belief." In *Lectures and Essays*. London: Macmillan, 1879.

Davidson, Donald. *Inquiries into Truth and Interpretation*. Oxford: Oxford University Press, 1984.

———. "On the Very Idea of a Conceptual Scheme." *Proceedings and Addresses of the American Philosophical Association* 42 (1974): 5–20.

Dennett, Daniel C. *Darwin's Dangerous Idea*. New York: Simon and Schuster, 1995.

Descartes, René. *The Philosophical Writings of Descartes*. Trans. John Cottingham, Robert Stootfhoff, and Dugald Murdoch. Cambridge: Cambridge University Press, 1984.

Dewey, John. *The Quest for Certainty*. New York: Minton, Balch, 1929.

Emerson, Ralph Waldo. *Essays and Lectures*. New York: Literary Classics of the United States, 1983.

Feyerabend, Paul. *Against Method*. 3d ed. London and New York: Verso, 1975.

Fogelin, Robert J. "Aspects of Quine's Naturalized Epistemology." In *The Cambridge Companion to Quine,* ed. Roger Gibson. Cambridge: Cambridge University Press, in press.

———. "Contextualism and Externalism: Trading in One Form of Skepticism for Another." *Philosophical Issues* 10 (2000): 43–57, 86–93.

———. "Hintikka's Game Theoretic Approach to Language." In *Philosophy of Logic: Proceedings of the Third Bristol Conference on Critical Philosophy (1974),* ed. Stephan Körner. Oxford: Basil Blackwell, 1976.

———. "Hume's Skepticism." In *The Cambridge Companion to Hume,* ed. David Fate Norton, 90–116. Cambridge: Cambridge University Press, 1993.

———. *Hume's Skepticism in the Treatise of Human Nature*. London: Routledge and Kegan Paul, 1985.

———. *Philosophical Interpretations*. New York: Oxford University Press, 1992.

———. *Pyrrhonian Reflections on Knowledge and Justification*. New York: Oxford University Press, 1994.

———. "The Skeptic's Burden." *International Journal of Philosophical Studies* 7, no. 22 (1999): 159–72.

———. "The Tendency of Hume's Scepticism." In *The Skeptical Tradition,* ed. Myles Burnyeat, 397–412. Berkeley and Los Angeles: University of California Press, 1983.

———. "What Does a Pyrrhonist Know?" *Philosophy and Phenomenological Research* 57, no. 2 (1997): 395–400, 417–25.

————. *Wittgenstein*. 2d. ed. The Arguments of Philosophers, ed. Ted Honderich. London: Routledge and Kegan Paul, 1987.

————. "Wittgenstein and Classical Skepticism." *International Philosophical Quarterly* 21 (March 1981): 3–15.

————. "Wittgenstein's Critique of Philosophy." In *The Cambridge Companion to Wittgenstein,* ed. Hans Sluga and David Stern, 34–58. Cambridge: Cambridge University Press, 1996.

Frede, Michael. *Essays in Ancient Philosophy*. Oxford: Clarendon Press, 1987.

————. "The Skeptic's Beliefs." In *Essays in Ancient Philosophy,* 179–200. Minneapolis: University of Minnesota Press, 1987.

————. "The Skeptic's Two Kinds of Assent and the Question of the Possibility of Knowledge." In *Philosophy in History*, ed. J. B. Schneewind, Richard Rorty, and Quentin Skinner. Cambridge: Cambridge University Press, 1984.

Grice, Paul. *Studies in the Way of Words*. Cambridge, Mass.: Harvard University Press, 1989.

Hegel, G. W. F. *The Phenomenology of Mind*. Trans. J. B. Baillie. 2d ed. London: George Allen and Unwin, 1931.

Hofstader, Douglas R. *Gödel, Escher, Bach*. New York: Vintage, 1989.

Hume, David. *Abstract*. In *Treatise of Human Nature*. Ed. L. A. Selby-Bigge and P. H. Nidditch. Oxford: Oxford University Press, 1978.

————. *Dialogues Concerning Natural Religion*. Ed. Norman Kemp Smith. London: T. Nelson, 1947.

————. *Enquiries Concerning Human Understanding and Concerning the Principles of Morals*. Ed. L. A. Selby-Bigge and P. H. Nidditch. 3d ed. Oxford: Clarendon Press, 1975.

————. *Essays, Moral, Political, and Literary*. Ed. Eugene F. Miller. Indianapolis: Liberty, 1987.

————. *The History of England*. 6 vols. Indianapolis: Liberty, 1983.

————. *A Treatise of Human Nature*. Ed. L. A. Selby-Bigge and P. H. Nidditch. 2d ed. Oxford: Oxford University Press, 1978.

James, William. *The Will to Believe and Other Essays in Popular Philosophy*. The Works of William James, ed. Frederick H.

Burkhardt et al. Cambridge, Mass.: Harvard University Press, 1979.

Jastrow, Joseph. *Fact and Fable in Psychology*. Boston: Houghton Mifflin, 1900.

Kant, Immanuel. *Critique of Pure Reason*. Trans. Norman Kemp Smith. London: Macmillan, 1953.

———. *Prolegomena to Any Future Metaphysics*. Trans. Lewis White Beck. New York: Liberal Arts Press, 1950.

Kuhn, Thomas. *The Structure of Scientific Revolution*. 2d ed. Chicago: University of Chicago Press, 1970.

Lewis, C. I. *An Analysis of Knowledge and Valuation*. LaSalle, Ill.: Open Court, 1946.

Lewis, David. "Elusive Knowledge." *Australasian Journal of Philosophy* 74, no. 4 (1996): 549–67.

Marcus, Ruth Barcan. "Moral Dilemmas and Consistency." *Journal of Philosophy* 77, no. 3 (1980): 121–36.

Middleton, Conyers. *A Free Inquiry into Miraculous Powers, Which are supposed to have subsisted in the Christian Church, From the Earliest Ages through several successive Centuries*. London: Manby and Cox, on Ludgate Hill, 1749.

Nehamas, Alexander. *Nietzsche: Life as Literature*. Berkeley and Los Angeles: University of California Press, 1998.

Nietzsche, Frederick. *The Portable Nietzsche*. Trans. Walter Kaufmann. New York: Viking Press, 1969.

———. *The Will to Power*. Ed. Walter Kaufmann, trans. Walter Kaufmann and R. J. Hollingdale. New York: Vintage Books, 1968.

Peirce, Charles S. *Collected Papers of Charles Saunders Peirce*. Ed. Charles Hartshorne and Paul Weiss. Cambridge: Harvard University Press, 1931.

Pinker, Stephen. *The Language Instinct*. New York: Perennial, 2000.

Plato. *Theaetetus*. Trans. M. J. Levett. In *The Theaetetus of Plato*, ed. Myles Burnyeat. Indianapolis: Hackett, 1990.

Quine, W. V. "Epistemology Naturalized." In *Ontological Relativity*, 69–90. New York: Columbia University Press, 1969.

———. *From Stimulus to Science*. Cambridge, Mass.: Harvard University Press, 1995.

———. *Word and Object*. Cambridge, Mass.: Massachusetts Institute of Technology Press, 1960.

Rorty, Richard. *Philosophy and the Mirror of Nature*. Princeton: Princeton University Press, 1979.

Sartre, Jean-Paul. *Existentialism*. Trans. Bernard Frechtman. New York: Philosophical Library, 1947.

Searle, John R. *The Construction of Social Reality*. London: Penguin Press, 1995.

Sextus, Empiricus. *Sextus Empiricus*. Trans. R. G. Bury. Loeb Classical Library. 4 vols. London: William Heinemann, 1961–71.

Sinnott-Armstrong, Walter. *Moral Dilemmas*. Oxford: Basil Blackwell, 1988.

Szymborska, Wislawa. *Sounds, Feelings, Thought: Seventy Poems by Wislawa Szymborska*. Trans. Magnus J. Krynski and Robert A. Maguire. Princeton: Princeton University Press, 1981.

Tarski, Alfred. "The Concept of Truth in Formalized Languages." In *Logic, Semantics, and Metamathematics*, 2d ed., 152–278. Indianapolis: Hackett, 1983.

Whitman, Walt. *Leaves of Grass: Comprehensive Reader's Edition*. Ed. Harold W. Blodgett and Sculley Bradley. New York: New York University Press, 1965.

Whorf, Benjamin Lee. *Language, Thought, and Reality: Selected Writings*. Cambridge, Mass.: Technology Press of Massachusetts Institute of Technology, 1956.

Williams, Michael. *Unnatural Doubts: Epistemological Realism and the Basis of Skepticism*. Oxford: Basil Blackwell, 1991.

Wittgenstein, Ludwig. *Culture and Value*. Ed. G. H. von Wright, trans. P. Winch. 2d ed. Chicago: University of Chicago Press, 1984.

———. *Notebooks 1914–1916*. Ed. G. H. von Wright and G. E. M. Anscombe, trans. G. E. M. Anscombe. Oxford: Basil Blackwell, 1961.

————. *On Certainty*. Ed. G. E. M. Anscombe and R. Rhees, trans. G. E. M. Anscombe. Oxford: Basil Blackwell, 1969.

————. *Philosophical Grammar*. Ed. R. Rhees, trans. Anthony Kenny. Berkeley and Los Angeles: University of California Press, 1974.

————. *Philosophical Investigations*. Ed. G. E. M. Anscombe and R. Rhees, trans. G. E. M. Anscombe. 3d ed. Oxford: Basil Blackwell, 1958.

————. *Remarks on the Foundations of Mathematics*. Ed. G. H. von Wright, R. Rhees and G. E. M. Anscombe, trans. G. E. M. Anscombe. 2d. ed. Oxford: Basil Blackwell, 1967.

————. *Tractatus Logico-Philosophicus*. Trans. D. F. Pears and B. F. McGuinness. London: Routledge and Kegan Paul, 1961.

————. *Zettel*. Ed. G. E. M. Anscombe and G. H. von Wright, trans. G. E. M. Anscombe. 2d ed. Oxford: Basil Blackwell, 1981.

INDEX

S